THE CUSTOMER SERVICE REVOLUTION

8 Principles That Will Change the Way Companies Think About the Customer Experience and the Employees Who Work for Them

Bryan Horn

authorHOUSE

AuthorHouse™
1663 Liberty Drive
Bloomington, IN 47403
www.authorhouse.com
Phone: 1 (800) 839-8640

© 2020 Bryan Horn. All rights reserved.

No part of this book may be reproduced, stored in a retrieval system, or transmitted by any means without the written permission of the author.

Published by AuthorHouse 02/19/2020

ISBN: 978-1-7283-4756-1 (sc)
ISBN: 978-1-7283-4757-8 (hc)
ISBN: 978-1-7283-4755-4 (e)

Print information available on the last page.

Any people depicted in stock imagery provided by Getty Images are models, and such images are being used for illustrative purposes only.
Certain stock imagery © Getty Images.

www.thecsrevolution.com

This book is printed on acid-free paper.

Because of the dynamic nature of the Internet, any web addresses or links contained in this book may have changed since publication and may no longer be valid. The views expressed in this work are solely those of the author and do not necessarily reflect the views of the publisher, and the publisher hereby disclaims any responsibility for them.

Praise for The Customer Service Revolution

"In this new book, Bryan sets the reader on a path of relatable stories and applicable methodologies to bring decency back to business environments! Bryan illustrates some of the craziness that drives business and that basic common sense should be the mantra. Enjoy the book! It's my pleasure to not only endorse this book but suggest you get it for your entire organization!"

—Jim Lally, President and Founder, Anaco Financial Group

"Bryan's wealth of experience provides practical and timeless advice to not only convince customers you want their business today, but you also want that customer to come back again and again. It's inspiring for all companies, regardless of product, service, or industry. Culture changing!"

—David Kitchen, Government / Public Services HR Director

"*The Customer Service Revolution* is truly an eye-opening read! Bryan has created a thought-provoking take on how to enhance the experience for the most powerful person on the planet—the customer. Reading this work reminds us of the power of the golden rule."

—Trevor Flisowski, Corporate Leadership and Service Training Professional

"Bryan successfully addresses the major issues concerning customer experience today. If you manage people and want customers to keep coming back with money in hand, this book is a must-read."

—Nick Brown, President and CEO, SalesCU

What a strange concept.....customer service is linked to employee satisfaction.

For my father ... I miss you.

Contents

Preface xv

Acknowledgments xix

Introduction xxi

Chapter 1
The Most Powerful Person on the Planet 1

- Spend an Extra Dollar; Feel Like a Million! 2
- Building Value and an Experience 4
- The Experience Economy 6
- Negative Customer Experience Recovery 8

Chapter 2
Aloha & Prego: Come in and Stay Awhile 13

- Prego Isn't Just a Pasta Sauce 15
- Impressions Last a Lifetime 16
- Creating an Inviting Space 18
- Aloha and Uber 20
- Every Customer Is a Guest 21
- Candidates and Aloha 23

Chapter 3
Putting Humanity Back in Human Resources 26

- Communication Is Key 27
- Being Humane and Human 29
- You Can't Leave Your Life at Home 30

- Risk Is More Than a Board Game 31
- It's Not Me, It's You! 32
- Seeing the Soul 35
- Know Your Worth 41
- Perks vs. Culture 43
- In This Together 45
- Fired for Doing Good 48

Chapter 4
Happy Employees, Happy Sales 51

- The Bill Lumbergh School of Management 59
- We're Just Employees 62
- The Best Coach Is Also the Water Boy 64

Chapter 5
Setting the Stage 67

- Perception of the Production 69
- Every Cast Member Deserves Applause 70
- Appearances Matter 72
- Everything Speaks 74
- The Little Things 78
- The Story within the Scene 83
- The Waiting Game 84
- Setting the Stage Behind the Scenes 86
- The Back-Office Problem 89
- Customer Service vs. Customer Experience 93
- Digital Customer Touch Points 95

Chapter 6
Thank You, Come Again! 101

- Give Customers a Reason to Come Back 101
- The Power of Yes 103

- I Have Always Wanted a Pony 106
- Nordstrom Sells Tires? 107
- My Pleasure 109
- Use Affirming Language 110
- I Will Remember You 111
- Get Creative 113
- Creating Unforgettable Moments for Customers 115

Chapter 7
Customer Service & Country Music 118

- Keep It Simple 121
- Take Pride in your Work 125
- Love What You Do 127

Chapter 8
Accountability: Working Together for the Good of the Customer 129

- It's Not My Fault 130
- Six Reasons for a Culture Void of Accountability 134
- The Customer Is Not Always Right 136

Afterword 143

Endnotes 145

Preface

"*DO YOU HEAR the people sing, singing the songs of angry men?*" Those are the iconic words from *Les Misérables*, one of the world's most beloved musicals. It is a song of revolution, the words of a people desperate for change.

Revolution is defined as "a sudden or radical change of perspective; an overthrow of a social order in favor of a new system."[1] If there has ever been a need for a revolution of the customer and employee experience, that time is *now*.

The world has changed. We hold computers in the palms of our hands. We can access real-time information within a matter of seconds. But with every innovation comes a radical change. Every industry in the world must reinvent itself with the dawn of the experience economy. We can now stay in people's homes, so why go to a hotel? With ridesharing, why call a cab? Why go out to your favorite restaurant when you can have food dropped off at your home? Why get out of bed and trudge down to the local department store when you can have everything delivered the same day *and* do it all in the comfort of your pajamas? These are the real challenges businesses face in this changing world. To stay competitive, a business must completely rethink how customers are treated.

Every revolution in history began somewhere. For this business revolution, it begins with the employees themselves. I firmly believe that the interaction I have with an employee reflects how an organization treats one. Many organizations are in desperate need of an overhaul if they hope *to stay in business* in this new era of *doing business*. The development of people is an integral part of the new experience economy.

I hold great respect for industry leaders such as CEOs, CFOs, and GMs. Many books about customer service are written from their perspective. And while I highly value those works, this is not one of those. It is written from the perspective of a frontline employee and manager. I feel confident in saying that I share the perspective of the many hardworking men and women out there who wish they could share these thoughts and concerns with the higher-ups. For these people, I hope you will see a little of yourself, your workplace culture, and your frustrations within these pages. I hope you will see a little bit of humor along with the commonsense approach I have tried to emphasize. I feel equally confident that I share the same frustrations about the customer experience as most consumers. I hope you will shout, "This has happened to me!" and can better understand how you have the power to change these interactions for the better.

If you are a manager, senior executive, or business owner, I hope you will take away some powerful and reflective points. I hope this work will allow you an opportunity to place yourself and your organization under a powerful microscope and examine closely its operations and culture. I hope a sincere reflection will provide chances to improve, refine, or reinvent how you conduct business. I hope you will come away with the perspective that the customer is the most powerful person on the planet, that they hold the fate of your entire organization in their hands, and that power should be respected. I hope most of all that you recognize the importance of employees, that they are human beings and need to be respected as such.

I will share with you my opinions backed up by industry leaders and scientific studies. I am in no way saying that what I am promoting is an industry doctrine. Rather, these are my thoughts and experiences based on more than sixteen years of management. I have been both a leader and a direct report. I have ended every chapter with a "bottom line", a small recap of the most important parts to take away from each section. I write from the perspective of someone who has managed others and who has been managed. I write from the perspective of a job searcher and candidate. I don't claim to know everything. I have a message to share and sincerely hope you see the intention in which it is being delivered.

Note to the Reader

The employee titles and employment status of individuals named may have changed since they were quoted by the original source. They were accurate at the time of the original quotation.

Acknowledgments

I SINCERELY WISH TO thank those who took time out of their busy lives to review this work. These individuals make up the best in their respective fields, namely human resources management, corporate training and development, financial management, and customer-service management. I am humbled by their kind words and praise for this project.

To the single mother who works two jobs just to put food on the table, thank you. To the father who works seventy hours a week and still has time to make it to his kid's baseball games, thank you. To the banking professionals I have had the pleasure to lead and serve, thank you. To the frontline managers who keep it all running, thank you. To the thousands of people behind the scenes who inspire both customers and employees daily with their acts of service, thank you. To the consumer who holds companies accountable and makes them strive for excellence every day, thank you.

To my friends who I consider family, you have been my source of strength and motivation. You have encouraged me and helped me to press forward. I love you all from the bottom of my heart.

Finally, to the people who are jobless and searching: hang in there! I have been where you are. I know what it is like. If anything, always know you have someone cheering on your success. If you are one unemployment check away from being evicted, or you are sitting alone and contemplating desperate measures, I want you to know that you are loved, you are valued, and you are needed. There is help. You got this! I am cheering you on every step of the way.

Introduction

I HAD AN EXPERIENCE at a big-box retailer (I shall not mention the name, but it is a retailer that can be found on virtually every continent on this planet). I was going on a camping trip and wanted a specific drink cooler. I went onto this retailer's mobile app, looked up the product in question, and verified that the store had several in stock. I forged my way through rush hour traffic after work, engaged in the daunting task of finding a parking space, and proceeded to enter the giant sliding doors. I walked clear back to the camping section, hoping this would be a seamless and quick experience. Lo and behold, no coolers! I looked for an associate. Whether or not you believe in religion, finding a sales associate at this store is nothing short of a miracle.

After several minutes of looking for said associate (and finally finding one), I asked where this item could be located. By the look on the young, uninformed clerk's face, you would think I was asking him to solve the Yang-Mills Existence and Mass Gap Equation (look it up ... if you can solve it, you win $1,000,000). The young clerk went to the back and was never seen or heard from again.

Long story short, and forty-five minutes later, it turns out the mobile app was wrong. There were no coolers in stock. It took forty-five minutes for someone to figure out that a cooler was not in stock! I reported this experience to a store manager with an official job description of "resolving customer concerns." I expressed my dissatisfaction at the mobile app giving incorrect information, with no available clerks to be found, the lack of concern from the one clerk I could find, and so on. This manager simply gave me a boorish "What do you want me to do about it?" response. So, I offered a compromise. There was a similar cooler that cost twenty-five dollars more than the one I was seeking. I requested I be sold that cooler for the price of the one I was looking for. That request was met with an immediate no, followed by a host of reasons why my request was outlandish. I walked out not only without product in hand but feeling even worse than I did before I walked in.

This is the distressing customer service culture that has invaded the world of commerce today. There is a pervasive "clock in, clock out" culture that has spread through the ranks of companies like a dangerous virus. Virtually every company has a mission statement about how important it is to take care of the customer. But is it enforced? More importantly, is it *lived and breathed* by a company?

In the good ole days, the customer was literally the heart and soul of a business. When a customer was not satisfied, companies bent over backward to remedy the error and win them back. The adage of "I will take my business elsewhere" does not have the same power it once did. Instead, it is met by companies with a "Fine. We don't need you anyway!" attitude. To the manager at the big-box shop, I was an inconvenience. But had that manager had a service mind-set, they would have seen me as a person having a very bad experience and an issue that needed to be remedied. A service mind-set would have looked for options, thought outside the box, and tried to redirect the negative experience to a positive outcome.

In a nerdy sort of way, I like watching customer-service training videos from companies. Maybe it is the bad acting or terrible scripts, but there is something mesmerizing about them. I watched a video from Nintendo in 1991 on YouTube for frontline employees at the then major retailer Circuit City. The narrator of the video gave several examples of potential problems customers might encounter when using a classic Nintendo system. The video was depicting a single mom bringing the gaming system back to the store because she could not figure out how to plug the controller in for her son. The narrator proceeded to say, "When a customer has a problem, they will come running to you! And that's a waste of time for everyone! You're not a Nintendo mechanic; you're a Nintendo customer-service specialist!" I respectfully contend that if you were a *true* specialist in customer service, the proper response would be, "Problem? Bring it on!"

Customer service needs to adapt and change. It is a scientific fact that consumers now are driven more by experiences than the product itself. Anyone can buy a product; the question is, can you get them to buy it from you *again*? In order to stay competitive, it is essential now more than ever to develop strategies to guarantee that experience and delivery are on par with the product or service being offered. If you ask most business owners how they deliver their product or service, they will probably mention the actual delivery channels in which its produced, namely through an internet site or brick-and-mortar location. They fail to mention the experience of the delivery channel as being equally crucial to the product or service itself.

Companies must revamp, redirect, and re-think how they are doing business if they hope to stay in business.

It is my hope that you will find these stories and lessons of advice useful. Creating the best possible experience for customers is my primary goal. It is what I do. It defines who I am. It is what I am passionate about. As products and services change over time, one thing will remain consistent: customers will always expect a magical and memorable experience. By allowing your employees to deliver those experiences, your customers will become your biggest brand advocates, and your sales will increase.

Chapter 1

The Most Powerful Person on the Planet

"There is only one boss: the customer. And he can fire everybody from the chairman down, simply by spending his money somewhere else." – Sam Walton

MY FATHER WAS A sales manager at a successful Tennessee car dealership. As a young kid, I watched him train his new sales staff. At the beginning of his class, he would put up three pictures: the president of the United States, the president of Russia, and an average working American man or woman. He would then ask his class, "Of these three people, which one is the most powerful person in the world?" Almost without hesitation, everyone would point to the president of the United States. My father would then say emphatically, "Wrong!" and proceed to take the picture down. He would ask the same question again, and everyone would point to the president of Russia, and again he would take the picture down. What remained was a common, ordinary person who, as my father explained, was the most powerful person in the world. And he was right.

Consumers have more power than they realize. They decide where they shop and for what. They decide which businesses keep their lights on and who gets to close shop. They decide how big something becomes and how reputable it is perceived to be. Big-box retailers who offer steep discounts are often criticized for their horrible service. So why do they keep getting bigger, with more locations built and more profit coming in? Because consumers decided it should be that way. Consumers can control the destiny, direction, and image of an organization through social media platforms and within the court of public opinion. The customer has untapped but very real power.

We are people of choice. We value our choices, our rights, and our freedoms. We passionately defend our freedom to keep and bear arms, our freedom to decide who we do (or do not) worship, our freedom to speak our minds openly, and so on. We also cherish our right to have choices in the marketplace, the very essence of capitalism. I can open a checking account at any bank or credit union and get a debit card. I can buy milk at just about any gas station or major grocery chain. I can sleep on any bed at various hotel brands. The difference is the experience I receive, and that experience is what will turn me into a brand ambassador and stay loyal to it.

Spend an Extra Dollar; Feel Like a Million!

Let's go back to the big-box retailer for a moment. I think it's fair to do a side-by-side comparison to illustrate this point. Here in the Salt

Lake City area, we have a chain of grocery stores that some might call elite. Let's put them up against each other and compare.

I walk into the big-box retailer, where if I am lucky, I may get a robotic welcome from some dear senior citizen. I may be able to find exactly what I am looking for quickly and efficiently. If not, I know I will be on the hunt for the next twenty minutes to find that bottle of window cleaner. If I am unable to locate it, I will be frustrated trying to find an associate who can point me in the right direction. The aisles, displays, and racks of merchandise will often be dirty, unorganized, and neglected. And then, by some act of Providence, I may get told "Thank you for coming in today" as I am paying for my items.

Let us traverse to the local supermarket. Upon walking in, I will be greeted by at least three front-facing employees with a warm and friendly smile. Interestingly enough, this particular grocery store chain builds and designs its stores so this can happen. No matter which of their sixteen stores you enter, the entrance is strategically placed next to a entrance-facing department (such as floral, pharmacy, or the deli) so that employees have no choice but to see you enter. Then, within a matter of moments, you will have a host of crew members fighting over who gets to take care of you and answer any questions you might have. They will never point to where you need to go; they will escort you there. I had one such experience when I was just picking up a gallon of milk, and the nice young lady walked me back, took it out of the cooler, and carried it up to the checkout. Now *that* is service!

You will find this store has clean aisles and organized displays. The floral department alone is like walking through a well-manicured botanical garden. The store lights are soft and don't make you feel like you're in a tanning booth. There will be quality and diverse options at the salad bar, and specialty items such as gourmet cheeses and artisan bread. It is a pleasant experience every time. Some give it this elite title because, yes, their prices are slightly higher. But they are offering a level of service that does not exist in many places. Yes, you are paying a dollar more for that gallon of milk. But the old saying of "you get what you pay for" is entirely true. Would you rather save a dollar and be made to feel like you are an inconvenience for spending your money, or would you rather spend an extra dollar and come out feeling like a million bucks?

Building Value and an Experience

In life, we are going to experience loss. It might be the loss of a loved one, the loss of a sentimental possession, or maybe even the loss of a job. People go through stages of grief and mourning no matter what type of losses they experience, and this is especially true when we must lose one of our most hard-earned commodities: money. We always feel bad when we must spend money. I don't know of one person who would honestly say, "I *love* to spend my hard-earned money on bills and groceries!" Okay, maybe a billionaire.

But I digress.

In sales, the first thing you do is build value in a product. You want others to know the benefits. When we trade in our cars, many feel some sentimental attachment to them. We have made memories in that car we are giving up. Maybe you took your firstborn child home from the hospital in that car. Maybe you took your future spouse on your first date in that car. Whatever the case, we attach sentimental feelings to inanimate objects. There is nothing wrong with that. It is just what we do as human beings. That is the first objection most sales professionals have when selling a car, a home, or something we have attached some emotional value to. They must build value in something new so when those feelings of grief and loss kick in, they are just as quickly circumvented with feelings of joy, pride, and happiness. In today's changing economy, value is not enough. An *experience* needs to accompany the actual product or service being sold.

I know that I *hate* to spend money. I will save it as long as I can. But when I do spend money, I want to feel appreciated. I have lost something that I didn't want to lose. The *least* someone else can do is soften the blow with a warm smile and a genuine "Thank you for your business." There are a few companies that truly understand the power of this principle. Sadly, many miss the mark. That is why I personally would rather spend an extra dollar to come out feeling like a million!

Dr. Art Markham of the University of Texas at Austin found the number one reason people experience some form of buyer's remorse is not because they could not afford an item. Rather, they regret the *experience* of buying it.[1] Dr. Markham further explains that humans have a set of brain patterns known as the avoidance and approach systems. The avoidance system sends us signals that cause us to take a step back and think, as if we are potentially being put in danger. The approach system, on the other hand, fights the avoidance system and tell ours brain, "Yeah, jump right in! Go ahead and live in the moment." It is a devil and an angel sitting on our shoulders, with one telling us what we want to hear and the other telling us just the opposite.

Most times, in the case of buying a car or a home, consumers are conscious of their budgets and payment. Remorse, or the avoidance system, kicks in after the fact when consumers start to reflect on the experience. Thoughts begin to enter our heads, like *Why did that salesman not show me that one page of the contract?* and *That salesman didn't even bother to shake my hand when I walked in!* The negative experience becomes the main thought, not the value in what we just purchased. That is why building the experience is at the core of building value.

The Experience Economy

Since the dawn of one-click checkout shopping and the millennial generation, we live in what is known as an experience economy. So much of what determines our purchasing habits stems from the experience in purchasing it in addition to the product itself. You're not just driving a luxury-brand car; now you're driving an *experience*. You're not just purchasing that Nicholas Cage pillowcase at 3:00 a.m. from your smartphone; you're purchasing an *experience*. You're not just taking out a second mortgage on your home to go to Disneyland; you're investing in an unforgettable *experience*. The approach system part of us screams in our ears because it knows remorse will soon kick in. The role of any good service-focused organization should be to mitigate the sense of remorse and loss with an unmatched *experience*. See the theme word developing? I know I have returned items, or didn't purchase them at all, when I have been made to feel bad for doing so. There have been several times, I have spent time gathering everything only to let it go and leave at the register because of the experience of handing over my money to an ungrateful employee.

Customers today are looking for genuine experiences. They will search far and wide for them. The sole purpose of an organization should be to empower employees to produce and provide those experiences. Companies today can still offer world-class service and life-changing experiences through adaptation and change to individual customer needs. Take the Ritz Carlton Hotel chain for example. The company is known worldwide for its distinct "Ritz style" of doing things. Certain key phrases, luxurious accommodations, and well-dressed individuals have all become synonymous with the brand. But in the mid-2000s, the company began to get some very vocal feedback concerning this experience from the younger generation. Millennials were not attracted to the white glove, napkin-over-the-wrist type of service their parents and grandparents were accustomed to. Micah Solomon wrote the following:

> Developing an authentic guest-service style is a requirement for success with customers in today's economy. Customers today, and younger customers in particular, are turned off by anything stilted or overly formal … their gut reaction to such a service style, even when it's delivered by the most caring providers in hospitality, is usually going to be negative.[2]

Today, having an experience has gone far beyond theme parks and entertainment attractions. The full interaction is now ingrained as part of the transaction. The personal nature, or lack thereof, is what is remembered. Every detail is measured as a reflection of the product or service offered. Customers want an all-encompassing experience that gives them a three-dimensional perspective. Customer participation is now critical to the experience process. They want to be a part of the service or product on which they are spending their hard-earned money. The Forum Shops at Caesars Palace in Las Vegas is a great example. If you have been there, you know it is a unique and memorable shopping experience. Shops are aligned down central streets to resemble the majesty and grandeur of ancient Rome. There are piazzas that direct shoppers centered with extravagant fountains and landscaping. Roman guards will walk, exclaiming "Hail, Caesar!" And as an icing on this already lavish cake, the Forum has a sky. The ceiling of this indoor wonder is painted with clouds and can even recreate thunder, lightning, and nighttime conditions. It evokes every sense of the human body. It truly is an experience to behold and is a great example of providing an all-encompassing experience for shoppers.

Negative Customer Experience Recovery

Every organization, big or small, is going to experience customer dissatisfaction. There are some people in the world you can never please. You can sweep all the leaves, and they're mad you didn't get every blade of grass. You give them the crust of the pie, and now they also want the crumbs. A service-focused organization, however, will have prepared for these moments, trained for them, and have procedures in place to remedy them at a moment's notice.

There are many issues that contribute to a bad customer experience. Some are outside of your control, such as an unforeseen weather pattern knocking your power out, or shipping issues through your carrier that delayed the arrival of a product. Some issues are just the result of being a human being. A steak will be over (or undercooked) at your favorite restaurant. Your sink will have an annoying drip at your luxury resort and spa. But these few and far between mistakes are easily forgiven. After all, we all make mistakes. But the issues that frustrate customers are the ones that are easily trainable and preventable. Issues like a call center agent showing absolutely no empathy or concern that we have been waiting for a lengthy period for assistance, or a frontline employee who gives you every reason under the sun as to why they can't resolve your concern rather than providing one reason why they can.

Customer-experience recovery is having a system in place to recover or, better yet, *redirect* the experience from a negative to a positive. May I suggest the following for a successful recovery after a negative customer experience:

- **Ask for forgiveness and validate the concern.** I am bothered when I express genuine concern in response to the negative service I have been given, only to be answered with, "I'm sorry you feel that way." Those are the death words of service recovery. What is being conveyed is that my concern is not valid, that the experience is just my perceived opinion of how things happened. And so it is not recognized, and it isn't real. A genuine "I am truly sorry that experience happened to you" goes a long way. You can even take it a step further and offer a small gift item in good faith. One thing I did as a bank manager was to keep themed gifts in my office for those few occasions I had an angry client. For example, I would keep several boxes of the board game Sorry! in the back room for those rare instances where I had to resolve an especially difficult concern. I, or a fellow banking professional, would hand the board game to the customer and simply say, "I am sorry for the experience you had with us." This small gesture conveyed that we genuinely regretted the experience or the perceived experience the customer had.

- **Empathize.** As I have said before, we are all humans. We all want to be treated as we hopefully treat others. We are all employees, and we are all customers. We have been in their shoes, and they have been in ours. A little understanding goes a long way. When a customer complained to me about something, nearly nine times out of ten, the same thing had happened at least once to me. I genuinely try to empathize with the customer and approach the situation from their perspective.

- **Explain circumstances.** There is a major difference between making excuses and explaining a circumstance. What's that old saying? "Excuses are like …? Everyone has one."

    I am sure you know the missing word here. But the verbiage is true. Sometimes there are circumstances beyond our control. And while we should still take ownership of the circumstance, we also owe it to our customers to give them the truth. I was one of millions of customers across the United States who were impacted by a series of severe winter storms several years ago that grounded major shipping companies in the middle of December. Like many others, I wondered if my packages would arrive for my loved ones by December 25. There was nothing these shipping companies could do. They were at the mercy of God. But I remember the brilliant way an employee at a local UPS Store explained it. As angry customers lined up, she stood up on the counter and said, "We are just as frustrated as you are that we cannot provide the service you have come to expect and deserve from us! For this, we apologize, and I will do whatever I can in my power to help!" Now, this young associate literally could do nothing. She did not have divine powers over time and space and could not just make all the snow disappear. What she did was explain the circumstance and not make a generic excuse. She said she would do whatever she could to try to help. I know for myself and many others that day, her offering to assist was just enough to calm our worries and make the situation just a little more bearable. By the way, a few days later, flights and delivery trucks resumed service nationwide.

- **Fix the problem.** This should seem like a no-brainer but surprisingly needs to be mentioned! What good is it to empathize and listen if you have no intention of resolving the problem? Provide real solutions and something to substitute the bad experience with a positive one. The online giant Zappos is amazing at this. I remember reading a story about a call center agent who assisted a customer with a return order. Introducing themselves as a "customer service resolution wizard," the agent sent the most amazing email ever, saying things like:

    > SHAZAM! Just like that, I have waved my magic wand and you have a 10% coupon flying through cyberspace to your email box for your next purchase with us! KAPOW! Another flick of my magic wand and your money will magically reappear in your bank account within 7 to 10 business days. POOF! Another flick of my wand and a return label is being delivered to your email box at this precise moment![3]

I mean, talk about taking it to the next level and turning a less than enjoyable experience into an amazing one! Resolving an issue should seem like common sense, but it is amazing how many companies do not genuinely offer to remedy the problem. They will say things like, "We will use this incident to train our employees to be better in the future." And that sounds great for you, but how does that remedy the situation for me, the customer? What did you do to genuinely try to earn my business back? Nothing. So, I will do exactly as you have requested through your actions and not come back at all.

- **Follow up.** The final part of successful customer service recovery is follow-up. When a customer expresses a genuine concern, take their information and set a time to follow up with them. Recap the concern and share with the customer what information you found out concerning the situation. Then share the outcome of what was done to resolve it. Finally, end with an offer to make it right. For example, offer a complimentary meal or replacement service next time the customer comes in. Offer an additional discount for the product or service for the inconvenience the customer experienced. If able, send a personalized thank you card or letter to the customer. These little acts speak volumes to how you value your customers when they express genuine concern and will help turn disgruntled guests into happy returning ones!

Bottom Line: The customer is the most powerful person on the planet. Respect this power and do not take your customers for granted. This is done with solid delivery systems and unmatched experiences. It is time for every organization and company in the world to realize the importance of this today and put it into actual practice.

Chapter 2

Aloha & Prego: Come in and Stay Awhile

"All are welcome here" – Dolly Parton at the grand opening of Dollywood in Pigeon Forge, TN

JUST THINKING ABOUT HAWAII conjures up thoughts of a beautiful woman placing flowers over your neck as you walk off the plane. Or maybe the smell of salt air mixed with gentle Pacific breezes and a cold drink in your hand. Or maybe it reminds you of the sincere and loving nature of the Polynesian people.

When a tourist visits Hawaii, virtually every airline, hotel, tour guide, and timeshare salesperson will at one-point mention "the spirit of aloha" in their motto, presentation, or logo. Why is this? Everyone knows that aloha means *hello* and *goodbye* in the Hawaiian language. But what many do not realize is that aloha is a philosophy of life embodied in a word. In fact, it is so important to Hawaiian culture that the laws of Hawaii actually mandate the government act in the spirit of aloha when conducting the business of the people.

The following is according to Hawaiian law:

> The Aloha Spirit is the coordination of mind and heart within each person. It brings each person to the self. Each person must think and emote good feelings to others ... "Aloha" is more than a word of greeting or farewell or a salutation. "Aloha" means mutual regard and affection and extends warmth in caring with no obligation in return. "Aloha" is the essence of relationships in which each person is important to every other person for collective existence. "Aloha" means to hear what is not said, to see what cannot be seen and to know the unknowable.[1]

I cannot recall one time being in Hawaii and *not* being approached by some random Hawaiian stranger and offered to be assisted, taken care of, or even invited over for dinner. Service is at the heart of the Hawaiian culture. Indeed, it is the lifeblood of many cultures around the world. Wouldn't it be nice if that same spirit was practiced by companies and organizations? How much more would commerce thrive if this culture of service was held to the same standard as growing the bottom line? What if we created an experience that not only caused returned business but also changed people's lives for the better?

Prego Isn't Just a Pasta Sauce

If you are one of the many fortunate people of the world who has ever been to an Italian house, then you will understand what *prego* means. Yes, it is a famous pasta sauce. But like aloha, it is a word used to convey a sincere spirit of welcome. It literally means, "I pray you ..." and then whatever you wish to happen. An Italian might gesture for you to come into their home and say, "Prego!"[2] It is a sincere indication that one is welcome to join, and all the stops will be pulled out to make the experience and time together the best it can be.

I would always make it a point to drive this point home with my employees. In fact, I would buy jars of the famous pasta sauce and put it at various teller stations or loan officer desks as a reminder to my staff. Some customers thought we were a little weird for having jars of pasta sauce in a bank, but it certainly got a conversation started!

We all get those vibes, those feelings in the pit of our stomachs or hairs on the back of our necks when we sense something is just not right. We have all been in a business where the musty chairs are just as uncomfortable as they look, or where a single person fails to acknowledge our presence. Think about walking into a luxury car dealership with marble floors, well-dressed individuals, and leather chairs. Now imagine walking into a used car lot on the side of the road with a run-down trailer and cars with rusted-out paint. Both examples set an expectation about the quality of the product sold and the level of service expected.

I think what we as humans fear the most is stepping outside of our comfort zones. Perhaps this is why the hospitality industry spends so much time and money on making people feel like they are at home—a place where they can relax, feel safe, and be themselves. As kids, we usually had some sort of safety blanket or stuffed animal.

Maybe your own kids always need to have their favorite blanket or toy in tow. For me, I always must bring my own pillow, no matter where I travel. I can't explain it, but there is something about having my own pillow that makes me sleep better at night. Hotels in some way or another strive to provide a feeling of safety, warmth, and comfort. People who go to hotels are generally displaced in some way. Perhaps a family is on vacation and is hundreds or thousands of miles away from home. Or an individual is going through a divorce and is transitioning homes. Another family might have just lost a home due to a fire or natural disaster and is awaiting insurance money so they can restart their lives. Whatever the case, a feeling of warmth and welcome is what is required. Yes, the hospitality industry is at the forefront of this (or at least they should be). But every industry can implement practices that invoke this same feeling of welcome. This is the spirit of aloha, the practice of prego in a service-driven organization.

Impressions Last a Lifetime

Let's take a page from the Disney handbook on the importance of creating a welcoming and positive first impression:

> When you first arrive at the main gates of Disneyland, you scan your pass and enter the park through the turnstiles. You are now in an outdoor lobby that features phones and restrooms. Once past the lobby, you walk into one of two short tunnels leading into Main Street's Town Square. The tunnels are lined with posters advertising the attractions within. As you leave the tunnels, even first thing in the morning, you

smell fresh popcorn, which is made in carts placed near the tunnel openings. The experience of entering the park is explicitly designed to remind guests of the experience of entering a movie theatre.³

From the onset, you know your experience is going to be something magical. Disney has designed it that way so that a guest will gradually build up excitement and anticipation. Now, I know that the excitement of going to a bank versus going to a place like Disneyland is at a very different level. But the point is the same. The first impression is the cornerstone of the entire experience and can be remembered for a lifetime.

When I was younger, I had a rare opportunity to attend Easter church services in New York City, followed by a lavish brunch at The Plaza Hotel located at the historic corner of Fifth Avenue and Central Park. Just the name of the hotel instantly evokes a feeling of luxury. Or it recalls Kevin McAlister asking Donald Trump for directions in the grand lobby in *Home Alone 2*.

I remember entering the lavish, ornate lobby adorned with gold accents and carpets that cost more than most American houses. I went into the dining room, where I felt as though I had stepped into where the queen of England eats her breakfast. The presentation of each food station made me feel bad for even touching, let alone eating it. It made such an impression on me that I thought, *I wonder if this is what it was like to dine on the* Titanic! This was the first and only time I got to experience The Plaza, but I will truly remember it with happy thoughts for the rest of my life. It is amazing to me how I still remember that some twenty-five years later. It is a testament to me of the power of setting an amazing first impression. No matter how big or small, your customers first impression of your business will be the one they remember and will be a contributing factor in deciding if they continue to do business with you.

Creating an Inviting Space

The saying goes, "You never get a second chance to make a first impression". First impressions are the key ingredients of making people feel welcome. I cannot tell you how many times I have walked out of a place of business because I did not feel welcome. Restaurants that have floors littered with food and dirty dishes don't exactly give us a warm and fuzzy feeling. Stores with disorganized shelves and mismatched inventory gives us a feeling of uneasiness. As people, we use all five senses to make decisions. If things *look* bad, we often think they *are* bad. If something smells wrong, we become defensive. If something sounds wrong, we put up our guard. All our senses are heightened when indicated of a potential problem. We take a moment to pause and assess the situation and make sure it feels right before we proceed. Therefore, first impressions are so crucial.

I went to a small local restaurant, and I remember leaving almost as fast as I entered. The place was a *disaster*. The paint was peeling off the walls, the seats were ripped and patched with tape, dead bugs on the ground and large amounts of dust piled up around the baseboards. The entire building had a weird chemical smell. No one welcomed me in and offered to show me to a table. Rather, a broken sign that read "Please seat yourself" was my hostess. I quickly got up and left. I knew it was a place I didn't want to spend my money. I thought at the time that maybe I was being overly judgmental. Maybe the food was perfectly fine. But something just seemed off to me. Turns out, this restaurant was shut down a month later for multiple health violations. It really didn't surprise me.

The first impression of your business reflects what you think of your customers. I could easily see that restaurant didn't value my business. The impression they conveyed was that I was not important enough to deserve a clean space. It was not welcoming. It did not scream to me that I was an invited guest. Rather, it did everything to push me away and make me want to never come back.

As a bank manager, one of my top priorities was making sure my location was always clean on the inside, while landscaping was manicured on the outside. Daily, I would often role-play being a customer and then see if the standards I set passed the test. The way you present your physical space reflects how you value your customers. Now I am not saying that a startup company or mom-and-pop shop should put in a glass chandelier or expensive toilet paper or provide the same amenities as a multimillion-dollar company. What I *am* saying is that little things make a difference. Broken-down, torn-up, and duct-taped chairs do not exactly send out the message of "Please sit your tired bottom down here and stay with us!" Old and rotting plants don't exactly ring out feelings of warmth and welcome. Rather, it sends a message that the customer is not worthy of a nice space, that no effort is made to create a feeling of welcome. If the customer is in an environment where they do not feel welcome, why should their hard-earned money be spent there?

One thing I am passionate about and is a very small expense to implement is having complimentary beverages (such as water, coffee, tea) and snacks available. This can be enhanced by a television showing relevant programming or even a DVD playing with appropriate selections. I once managed a bank branch where a selection of Disney movies played every day. Not only did the kids love it, but employees loved having branch sing-along contests with the customers and their children, often with the rewarding of a candy sucker to the best singers (which were always the kids).

Aloha and Uber

Not long ago, I lost my job at a local financial institution, a story which I will share later. To make extra income, I began to drive for the popular rideshare service Uber. When I first began, I had no clue what I was doing and was often nervous to take complete strangers in my personal vehicle. I did nothing special to enhance the rider experience. I just picked them up and took them to where they wanted to go. Simple as that. Well, my lackluster level of service showed. My driver ratings were mediocre. I would receive a small tip here and there. So, I completely redesigned the experience for my riders by becoming one myself. I switched roles and thought of the things that would make me want to give this driver a nice tip or leave a positive review. I decided to transform my simple car ride into as much of a luxurious experience as possible. I made it a practice to open the door for each passenger as they entered and exited the car. I dressed up nicely. I purchased bottled water and a host of snacks and put them in a nice basket in the back seat (there's that inexpensive touch again). I placed a nice selection of magazines and newspapers in the backseat pockets, along with tissues, hand sanitizer, and charging cords for cell phones. I purchased a plan on my phone that would turn my phone into a portable Wi-Fi hotspot so passengers could use their laptops or tablets during their rides. I put nice towels down on the floors to keep the space clean. I always kept a car air freshener inside. I made conversation. Within a few rides, the experience was night and day. Passengers were enthusiastically complimenting me on how their ride was the best Uber experience on the planet! I even put in a karaoke system for when I did bar runs so that passengers could have some fun on the way to or from their bar of choice. That led to some *interesting* rides!

My tips increased, and people began leaving comments on the Uber app about the level of service I offered. I wanted people to feel valued, and the people responded. Soon, I was handing out business cards. Passengers who used the service regularly would call me in advance and make appointments for me to take them to the airport or a special event downtown. I did nothing special but go a little above and beyond to provide a memorable experience. These were simple things but proved successful in standing out from the competition.

Every Customer Is a Guest

I treat every customer as my guest rather than the source of my paycheck. When you view your customers as welcomed guests, the spirit of aloha just seems to naturally rise to the surface. You want to make these people feel important. You want to impress them. You want them to come back. And in turn, your customers will feel that spirit. They will want to feel all warm and fuzzy. They will want to drive out of the way and wait in line for that specific bank teller who always remembers their name and genuinely takes interest in their concerns. They will want to spend an extra dollar to come out feeling like a million.

I firmly believe we become what we surround ourselves with. I am not perfect, but I try my hardest to create the aloha spirit for those I work with and those customers I serve. Polynesian cultures, along with many others of the world, surround themselves with beliefs that encourage cooperation, gratitude, and respect. The popular customer-relationship management (CRM) software company Salesforce understands this principle. Sarah Boutin explains:

> Aloha is an outlook that emphasizes the importance of interacting kindly and honestly with those around us. Aloha comes to life through the way our employees genuinely connect with each other and our customers and bring their whole, authentic selves to work.[4]

Yes, the customer is your source of income. They put money in the pocket of the business or service provider. The difference, however, is treating your customer as a means to an end versus a valued and welcomed guest. It is all a mind-set. I believe that my customer is my guest because without them I cannot survive. This is especially true in commission-based industries such as car sales. I have seen both incredibly bad and exceptionally good examples of this. I have purchased cars from snake oil salesmen, and I have purchased cars from valued and trusted friends. As a senior director of auto finance, I sincerely endeavored to bend over backward to help my customers feel like valued guests. I felt humbled and honored when customers would buy additional products from me, and in turn, I would receive a nice commission afterward. Without them, I take home nothing. No money goes into my pocket. So, I want to roll out the red carpet for them. I want them to walk away knowing they are appreciated and respected. I want them to come back and do business with me again.

Candidates and Aloha

This spirit of welcome should also extend to potential employees. To borrow yet another page from Disney, consider their belief in creating this spirit of welcome for potential employees. I feel it best to have them tell the story about the construction of their HR operations center:

> The Walt Disney World Casting Center was designed by renowned architect Robert M. Stern, who immediately understood the power that the finished building would have to impress potential cast members. A human resources center, as explained by Stern, "may be the only time you experience the total identity of the corporation. It's very important, symbolically." Accordingly, he created an entry point to the organization that is described as "otherworldly and fanciful, as if it had dropped from the pages of a picture book; a stop-frame of an animated film." As prospective cast members enter the doors, they grasp door-knobs patterned after the talking doorknobs in the film Alice In Wonderland. As you travel up to the second floor where the receptionist awaits, you get a symbolic tour of the company through hallways and rotundas of ever-changing shapes and perspectives. Gilded figures of cartoon characters sit atop columns, scenes from Disney animated films are painted on the walls and ceilings. This was all done to invite the potential cast member to "wander and be amazed!"

Let them get a taste of what it means to be a part of something magical![5]

Were you just as impressed by this as I was? Again, I am not saying by any means that you must spend millions of dollars to welcome a candidate in this fashion. Disney certainly has the resources to build something of this magnitude. What costs us *nothing* is the application of aloha, that genuine conveyance of welcome to all.

When I learned this principle, it made me rethink and reform the experience my candidates for various bank jobs had with me. I admit I used to just take them into a back room or office, sit them down, and engage in mundane questions. But after reading this, I sat down and asked myself if I was conveying a message of aloha, that I *want* you to join our work family. Were my actions saying, "Prego! You are welcome here!"?

So, I made small changes to my interview process. I received clearance to ask my own questions and not the scripted "If you could be any animal ..." or "Do you have any special skills?" questions usually given by the HR department. I would walk the candidate around the office, introduce them to all the people who worked there, and offer them water or coffee. If it was for a higher-ranking position or one that required more experience in a particular area, I would try to take the candidate out for coffee or lunch or meet at a park in a more relaxed environment. Regardless of the candidate, I would ask them about their dreams, their interests, what they hoped to be in life both professionally and personally. Next, I would be transparent about my expectations and convey that I expected the candidate to do the same. I would then end with the next steps and give realistic time frames about the process. Even if they were not the best fit for the role, I believed then and now that they deserved to feel welcome and that they knew I appreciated the time and energy they spent in preparing for the interview.

Bottom Line: When you invite a friend or family member over to your home, do you often go the extra mile to make sure things look just perfect upon their arrival? Do you make sure your flowers are watered, the porch is swept, and the window shades are dusted? Do you put together some tasty snacks and a refreshing pitcher of a mutually favorite drink on the coffee table? If you are like me, you want to make a great first impression. You do "little things" (I will be using those two words repeatedly later) that your guest may not see but that will ultimately enhance their time with you. I know for myself I like to make sure things are just right. Part of it might be my obsessive-compulsive nature, but I am committed to making sure my guest knows they are welcome. I feel proud when my guest(s) have a smile on their face after a nice home-cooked meal, or when they say, "You didn't have to go to all this trouble just for me!" And the truth is they are exactly right. I didn't have to do any of those things. I could have put homemade spaghetti on some paper plates and used cheap napkins and plastic silverware, and I know my guest would have been just as happy. But I want them to know that I value them, their friendship, and their taking time to visit me. They could have visited anyone else in the world, but they chose me. I want to go above and beyond because I value them. I want to set a stage (you will hear that again too) for them. The same is true for customer service. To repeat from earlier, the customer is the most powerful person in the world. You want to make sure they have a great experience and return again. This is what we should always have in the back of our minds with each touch point and interaction.

Chapter 3
Putting Humanity Back in Human Resources

"Be a good human being, a warm hearted, affectionate person. That is my core belief." – The Dali Lama

I MUST PREFACE THIS chapter by saying every book I have ever picked up regarding customer-service development has a Hail Mary chapter, meaning a chapter that is a long shot away from relating to the overall theme, but the author felt it was important enough to mention it in their work. Well, this is mine. I must disclose that I am by no means a human resource professional. I am not even an amateur! What I do know is that a substantial part of a successful service-driven culture is developing the culture of the workplace. That is why this chapter, as well as the next, will focus primarily on workplace culture and people development.

With that in mind, we begin.

When I think of modern human resources, I synonymously think of *The Terminator* movie, and three words come to mind: artificial, robotic, and emotionless. The human aspect of human resources is all but lost. In the good ole days of business, human resources were the essential driving force in employee development. Susan Schmitt, senior vice president of HR for Rockwell Automation, states the following:

> As an HR professional, you just can't be a manager advocate, shareholder advocate or company advocate to the detriment of the employee. The employee is the spirit and soul of the company.[1]

Human resources now consist mainly of job postings, recruiting, explaining a benefits package, and onboarding. But what about motivating and developing the actual human? What about career advancement, succession planning, and additional training? What about recognizing their personal needs as people?

Communication Is Key

The driving force behind good management is the art of communication. How you address and talk to people is more important than the amount of money your department brings in or if a quota deadline was met. Frontline managers expect HR to do that, while HR expects frontline managers to do it. Communication is lacking; a partnership is essential. Frontline managers have the most interaction with their direct reports, whereas HR has a few key touch points. HR should strive to make the most of those key interactions with the partnership of management.

When having to discipline an employee, I always used as much kindness as possible to soften the inevitable blow about to follow. There are certain steps I would follow.

First, I would always recognize the employee's talents. Everyone, no matter what role or capacity, has a unique set of talents that have contributed to your organization. Maybe the guy who cleans the floors is the best darn floor cleaner out there. Maybe the person who shreds your sensitive documents is the best darn paper shredder on the planet. No matter who they are, everyone has a gift.

Second, I would complement them on the things they had done right and how those contributions boosted the organization. This aspect to me is the *most* important. Almost every employee I have had to coach, discipline, or sadly terminate has expressed to me their appreciation for pointing out the good in them. So often, it is in our nature to criticize, judge, and see the worst in others. When that dreaded "I need to see you in my office" memo comes in from the boss, instantly our stomachs start to hurt, and we expect the worst. I have had many employees tell me that the kindness and compliments I offered were what made the news I had to share tolerable.

Third, I would transition carefully. For example, I would say something like the following: "Mr. Employee, it is because you are such a good bank teller that I am a little concerned with something that occurred yesterday. It has come to my attention that you cashed an obviously fraudulent check on someone's account. This is not like you to make a major mistake like this. Can you explain the circumstances a little better so I can understand what happened here?"

The above dialogue is almost a verbatim conversation I had with a real employee of mine. This sounds a lot better than "You really are stupid! How could you make such a mistake?" Sadly, this kind of pontificating style is all too prevalent and points to how we have disconnected the human element from human resources.

Being Humane and Human

Many organizations believe that if they provide water, breaks, and bathroom facilities, they are treating their employees humanely. Yes, that is technically true. But, is it being *human?* Maslow discussed the most basic of needs for humanity to survive. Our innermost need to feel appreciated, welcomed, needed, and valued is at the top of the list. The first humans on this planet established societies based on strong communal principles. Everyone had a place and a purpose. When the cavemen didn't want someone around, they made it very clear they were not welcome through shunning, discrimination, and even killing the person. As we have evolved, our most basic primal instincts have carried down through more than two thousand millennia of prosperity. We still have a yearning to belong somewhere, to be needed, and to feel appreciated. We crave it. We long for it. We even fight for it.

HR departments have genuinely disconnected from human development or interaction. Maybe the reason for this is that it is easier to pretend to care rather than actually caring. It is easier, more convenient and time-efficient, and better to the bottom line to be robotic. It is emotionally safer to manage through a predetermined set of procedures rather than take the time to understand someone's dreams, hopes, and desires. And even harder is possibly admitting mistakes and implementing the necessary changes to corporate lifestyles.

You Can't Leave Your Life at Home

We can make requests of employees, and even ourselves, to leave home life at home. But let's face it. We would be no different than the Terminator robot ourselves, void of all emotion, empathy, and reality. I feel confident in saying that every manager who preaches "leave your home life at home" is themselves guilty of breaking this rule.

Things are going to come up. Life is going to happen. It is a fact. It is about how leaders deal with those situations and making sure companies have programs in place to assist. I heard of a call center organization that had a "phone a friend" service. It was made up of fellow employees but was anonymous. The company actually paid these individuals to take time off their normal work schedules and be available for fellow employees to simply talk to. None of these employees made extra money for doing so. Instead, it was a positive outlet for employees who were struggling with work or home issues. They also had a list of company resources, such as an employee-assistance program, as well as external resources that could be referred for additional help. This is just one example of a company going the extra mile to put the human element back in human resources.

In this new economy, it is unreasonable to expect people to not bring some element of their personal lives to work. You are not hiring a chair warmer but living and breathing human beings. People are going to have sick kids or be sick themselves. They are going to need to leave early to see their son play baseball or their daughter's piano recital. They are going to need some time to unwind and pursue passions outside of a work setting.

Now, I am in no way advocating that a company should tolerate excessive excuses for low performance or tardiness. After all, the employee is there to do a job and collect a paycheck. What I am advocating is that instead of writing up standard disciplinary notes for the employee file, why not try to get to the root of the issue? Sometimes an employee has some very difficult life circumstances that will come into major conflict with the needs of the employer. The role of an employer is not to be a therapist, a problem solver, or a life coach for an individual. The organization must be a good steward of everyone involved. As Mr. Spock said on *Star Trek*, "The needs of the many outweigh the needs of the few." However, there can be a balance. Since we spend more time at work than at home, why not try to make that time as productive as possible? Let's start treating people like people. If you need to leave early, then go ahead, if it is not a chronic practice or abused. You need time off for a doctor's appointment? Then go ahead and take it! You need to work from home for a day or two while your kids are sick? Make it happen! What many corporate cultures have done is infantilized the employee experience. Many workers feel they need to apologize for having a personal life. If customers are happy, I am happy. If the product is moving or services are being rendered, I am happy. Happy employees results in great service, which leads to brand loyalty and return business. It's that simple!

Risk Is More Than a Board Game

I am not an HR professional, and perhaps that is why I don't understand this whole concept of not taking risks on people. Any business profits when it takes appropriate risk. I look at the movie industry as a great example. *The Poseidon Adventure*, *Star Wars*, *The Exorcist*, and *Gone with the Wind* were all once threatened with being shut down or not being green-lighted at all due to risk. Someone told George Lucas that his ideas were insane, unproductive, and childish. David O. Selznick was told *Gone with the Wind* would be the biggest failure of all time with Vivien Leigh and Clark Gable as the lead roles. Irwin Allen had to borrow $4 million from personal friends to finish *The Poseidon Adventure* because the production studio said his movie was full of risk. I personally think that HR professionals need to uncheck some of the must-haves and open their minds a little to a world of possibility associated with risk. Picking a candidate for a job is like electing one to political office. I don't know of any person on any political spectrum who would agree a candidate has everything they are looking for as a voter. So why do we hold the same standard for workplace candidates? Do you remember when you were hired at your first job, or maybe the job you are at now? Do you ever stop to think, *Wow, someone must have taken a major risk on me at one point*. So, why not take a risk on someone else?

It's Not Me, It's You!

It has been my experience that job hunting is a lot like dating: awkward, full of mixed messages, and rejection. It's like when the social reject of the school is set up with the most popular boy or girl, asked to prom, and then left alone on the couch, dressed up with nowhere to go. It is a heartbreaking and often emotionally draining experience.

I have been like millions of others who get those automated "thanks but no thanks" emails. And to be honest, they make me incredibly angry. Granted, I understand that some companies have maybe hundreds of applicants and can't respond to every single one personally. But most companies do have the time and resources to send a personal letter. They just *don't*.

So, what is really being said in those emails? This is by no means an expert opinion but rather my own personal one through experience. Let's translate.

- "We will keep your résumé on file" means your résumé is buried in the same place the ark was at the end of the first *Indiana Jones* movie. It is tucked away, safe from any prying eyes. This is also a way for a company to say "please don't apply here again" for a different position. Why? We have your résumé on file, after all!

- "We chose someone whose talents and experiences are more in line with our company needs" is the one that gets me boiling angry because it is so far from the real truth. It means that they wanted their friend or family member for the position, despite a no-nepotism policy. It means they went with someone with *fewer* qualifications and skills who could be hired to do the same job for less money. It means they looked you up on Facebook or other social media and saw something they didn't personally like, which could even be a Title VII violation, and just hid behind a generic statement. This is why I believe if you're going to have a social media account, use a fake name for the real you and your real name for the professional you. Sadly, we live in a world where judgment is dished out before learning any facts. We may see a candidate on social media who supports a political candidate that we strongly oppose and just assume they must not be hirable. Or, we see someone who is not religious and is perceived as dishonest or untrustworthy. Whatever the case, judgment is cast.

- "You have an impressive set of skills, but unfortunately …" really means that someone is too afraid to tell you the *real* reason, which again might be something that, if told, could be illegal. We know better, however. If we have impressive skills, why are we not even getting an interview? Common sense would dictate to us that if I am impressive, you would want to get to know me. So then why did your system decline my résumé just as fast as I submitted it? Do you not want impressive people to work for you?

And the *worst* rejection is the one you don't get at all. You have sent follow-up emails and made calls—yet nothing. It is incredibly frustrating and even downright rude. This is a major area where humanity has been removed from human resources. This is where companies and professionals have forgotten that there is a real person on the other end of the computer screen, hoping for some closure.

So, how can HR professionals put humanity back in human resources when it comes to rejections? I offer the following pieces of advice:

1. *Be respectful.* Please refrain from saying, "We've gone in another direction." People see right through it.
2. *Be direct.* Please do not soft-pedal the answer. Provide an explanation. Remember that you don't know what possible severe financial, familial, and emotional hardships the candidate is facing. The least you can do is exercise truth. You are giving a profound gift when you provide answers. And if it makes you uncomfortable, then may I suggest finding a new

career path? You are in the humanity business, the business of working with people, after all.

3. *Be professional.* Be responsive and communicate with candidates and employees. Technology makes it possible to connect in seconds, from any location, and in a variety of ways (e.g., phone, email, text, Instagram, LinkedIn message, etc.). There are 168 hours in a week. It takes a few minutes of your time. I know it is hard to do this in every situation, but it can be done in most.

4. *Be mindful.* Please treat everyone as you expect them to treat you. It's called the golden rule, that thing we all learned in preschool. Instead of telling someone how they are not qualified, how bad they are, why not try commending them on their strengths and give recommendations for the future? Why not try to genuinely *help* the person rather than add to their already mounting emotional and financial stress? Call it karma, call it fate, but remember what goes around comes around. One day you could find yourself in a similar situation.

Seeing the Soul

I asked a friend of mine, who is the HR director for one of the largest and fastest-growing cities in the state of Utah, to elaborate on this topic. He answered that he tries to see people humans first. He further reflects on how he endeavors to treat the candidate at the end of the conversation like a real person. He is passionate in the belief that all people are to be respected. He has a personal rule that if he interviews a candidate, they at least deserve a call back if they were not offered the position. Yes, it is inefficient sometimes, but it's the right thing to do. To him, the genuine human concern is a far better ROI than lip service and a lack of empathy.

Many human resources professionals have completely forgotten that there are real human beings on the other end of the phone or the computer, humans who are possibly desperate for work, hoping that a miracle will occur, and will be extended an offer. They are real people who might be one day away from defaulting on rent or a mortgage, or who might already be homeless. Humans who might be so bogged down with financial and emotional trauma from being unemployed, or underemployed, that they are considering desperate measures. These are the things I personally believe we have lost as a corporate society, the little thoughts that should fill our minds.

In banking, there is an industry practice that governs lending compliance: if your mother was sitting in front of you, would you go ahead and do it? It is a guideline for lenders to think twice about manipulating the situation to their benefit, knowing it could potentially hurt the person in front of them.

I challenge HR professionals to put this into practice. If your mother was sitting in front of you applying for the job, or better yet, if you knew they were at the other end of the computer, would you treat them the same way as other candidates? Would you just forget to send any kind of update email? Would you treat them with more compassion and humanity than a total stranger? Would you offer them feedback? Would that person become different in your eyes?

I now share with you a very personal story, the inspiration for this book. It is very close to my heart and one I have not shared with many people. But since it is relevant to seeing the soul of a person, I will share it with you.

The Customer Service Revolution

Several years ago, I fell into rough times and became homeless. Living in hotels, friends' houses, and even my car, it was a time that tested every ounce of faith and hope I had. It is not relevant to go into the details of how this came to be. But it was due to no fault of my own. It was not because I was addicted to drugs or led a life of crime. Rather, it was due to some unfortunate life events. With that said, I actively worked to better myself. I refused to let my circumstances get the better of me. I refused to wallow in the victim mentality, even though many people have told me I had every right to. I continued to fight for what I knew to be right. I worked hard but always seemed to catch the short end of the stick.

I had taken a job as a branch manager of a local credit union. I shall not mention their name, for doing so would give them undeserving attention. I thought it was the turnaround moment for my career. I thought that career move would be the end of climbing the mountain, and I could finally ease down into a peaceful valley. I was terribly wrong.

I got right to work. I revamped the service culture of the branch from that of mediocrity to customer focused. I dove into the local business community, trying to revive old contacts and make new ones. I actively sought out loans to increase revenue. In a matter of forty-five days, I had closed more than $137,000 in new lines of credit—pretty good for someone on the job just a little over a month! Little did I know that behind the scenes, things were going downhill for me fast. It was right in front of me, but I failed to see it.

A fellow employee defined herself as an *empowered feminist*, meaning she believed she did not have to listen to any authority other than her own. She was young and immature in the business sense. She openly refused to listen to anything I directed her to do. However, despite this clearly defiant attitude, she felt she deserved a promotion. I was more than willing to consider such a request, but I informed this young lady that I would need to see some corrective performance and knowledge of lending practices before I would even consider the idea. That was not an acceptable answer for her. Within days after sharing my concerns with her, I was accused of making racist statements to this individual. I never did anything of the sort and knew this was direct retaliation for not promoting her on the spot. Despite an investigation completely clearing me of any wrongdoing, this lit a fire that quickly grew out of control.

A few days later, my direct supervisor approached me and said we needed to have a serious discussion. She stated to me that she had been made aware that I was homeless, and she demanded an explanation as to the circumstances. It proceeded to be a two-hour interrogation and the most dehumanizing experience I have ever had. I was told that homeless people are liars, thieves, and addicted to drugs. I was informed of her concerns that I had access to large amounts of money. She made a general assumption about homeless individuals and made an egregious, stereotypical assessment of me. I felt as though I was the defendant in a jury trial having to passionately explain my housing status.

Despite my best efforts, I lost the battle. A few weeks later, and a week before Christmas coincidently, this same individual walked into my office without any warning and informed me that I was terminated. When asked if it was due to my homeless status, the response was, "I have concerns, and now I am addressing them." Officially, I was terminated for the offensive comments I never in fact made, which was confirmed in the investigation that cleared me of any wrongdoing. Unofficially, I knew it was because I was homeless.

Up until that time, I was what you would call a man's man—tough and afraid to show my feelings. However, that single experience broke down every perception of masculinity I had. I wept like a baby, for days in fact. I suffered debilitating depression and anxiety and still do as a result. That first night, I strongly considered suicide. I did not see the need to go on in this life. I could not handle the tremendous and unspeakable pain I was in. I thought to myself how amazing it is that someone can destroy your goals, your dreams, and your life in a matter of seconds. I found it wrong that a person of this low moral caliber was in a position of power and making great money, yet I was homeless and jobless. It did not seem fair.

I sat alone in a freezing car with a loaded gun, thinking to myself how best to end my suffering. The thought of being at peace was a tranquil thought. Deep down in my heart, I did not want to die. I just wanted my pain to end. I remember looking up into the night sky, convinced there was no God who could possibly love me. How a loving God could allow such evil in the world was beyond me.

Somehow, I made it through that night. But my depression worsened over the next few weeks. Being terminated a few days before Christmas combined with having no family is a dangerous set of emotional combinations. I turned to heavy drinking. I spent Christmas alone in a hotel room. It was my Christmas gift to myself. Every night, I cried until I could cry no more. Thoughts of suicide raced through my head at every available moment. I truly thought there was no light at the end of the tunnel. The path had ended, and there was nothing but a giant precipice before me, emotionally and professionally speaking. It was Christmas night when I wrote out a long suicide manifesto for someone to find upon my departure. I outlined how this company had taken my life, how they were guilty of murder in my eyes, questioning how they could do this to a fellow human being. I explained how this lone act of selfishness on my part would be revenge for what they did. I sealed the letter in an envelope, and then something amazing happened. Call it a voice from God, call it my own conscience, call it whatever you will. But an overwhelming feeling came over my heart and mind. A certain feeling poured through my entire body. I cannot describe it, but it was a "you will rise above this" kind of feeling. Somehow, I knew that I had to get back on track. I knew the greatest revenge I could ever bring was to be successful and rise above. My death would mean nothing to this direct supervisor or the credit union she represented. She would feel no remorse because she had no soul. She lacked any human emotion, and that is why she could sleep at night knowing what she did. My death would mean nothing, but my resurrection from this dark place would drive her mad. That is exactly what I wanted.

And so, I began to write this book. I began to channel all my thoughts, my feelings, my hopes, my dreams, and my frustrations. At first, it was going to be a work for me and only me. But I felt as though I had a purpose, a unique perspective that had to be shared. I dedicated all my effort into making my dreams come true. It has not been easy. Would I want to go through it again? I honestly cannot say. On the one hand, it was the worst time of my life. On the other, it was the catalyst for me to completely redefine my path and my purpose.

As you read on, the message I hope you take away from all of this is that we are all human beings. We all deserve kindness. We all deserve respect. The world is a tough place. The odds are generally not in our favor. The cards are usually stacked against us. I am not saying that you must like everyone or be everyone's friend. Some people are just difficult to get along with. But simple acts of kindness go a long way. Humanity transcends every race, religion, creed, and color. And this is especially true in the workplace.

Had I been seen as a human, I sincerely believe the outcome of this particular story would have been very different. But for whatever reason, this organization chose to foster a culture that does not share a positive outlook on humanity. They chose to retain and hire individuals who are toxic and even downright cruel. To them, I was a piece of garbage that needed to be eliminated as soon as possible. Therefore, I feel so strongly that if employees are treated as respected colleagues, they will deliver exceptional service. And as a result, sales will skyrocket. It is a very simple formula for success.

I don't claim to have some high moral code. I just believe in doing things right the first time and being accountable for mistakes when they occur. I believe in treating employees and customers the best I can, and I look for opportunities to serve. I don't share this story for attention or compassion. I share this experience with the sincere hope that what happened to me will never happen to another fellow human being. I understand and agree that a human resources department is crucial to protect the company and its interests. But I ask that the soul of a human be seen, not the generic and often nonexistent checklist used to evaluate potential.

Know Your Worth

I believe one of the greatest television series in history was the NBC hit *Wings*, running from 1990-1997. It was *Cheers* in an airport, following a group of friends/co-workers at the fictional Tom Nevers Airport in Nantucket, MA. Among the characters was Roy Biggins portrayed by the talented David Schramm. Roy was the definition of a boorish, sexist, and insecure man. He was the owner of Aeromass, the only other airline on the small vacation island and direct competitor to the other main characters. He was deceptive in his business practices. Despite being well known in the community as a member of the

Nantucket City Council, he is known amongst his peers as incredibly dishonest, often stealing tips from the struggling lunch counter operator and unfairly discriminating against airline passengers with outlandish ticket prices. He reveals that he established a false charity for his late wife (who turned out to be alive) and used the proceeds to go fly fishing in Maine and purchased a subscription to the *Playboy Network*.

The 1994 episode *Moonlighting* finds the group discussing odd-jobs they worked during Nantucket's cold and tourist-lacking off season. While the other businesses struggle, Roy's is doing quite well despite the lack of tourist revenue. When asked, he reveals his secret: demoralize his employees so badly that eventually they become convinced they will never amount to anything in life, and will accept the fact the best job they can ever have it at Aeromass. Then, when they have this realization, Roy cuts their pay in half and they are appreciative for something rather than nothing. Coming from a fictional television series, it is rather funny. In reality, it is a horrible company culture.

Humanity has never responded well to being treated as less than what it was destined to be. When humanity is stripped away, something ugly can emerge. Humans need to feel included, respected, and have a purpose in life. These feelings are the foundation of our nature as a species. Maslow confirmed that. I sincerely would have hoped by the dawn of 2020, organizations would have evolved away from the management style of Roy Biggins, where employees are considered sub-human robots that are programmed to make a profit. But sadly, it has gotten worse. Many organizations not only keep this disposable mindset about their employees, but also their customers. What is so tragic is that thousands of employees are just like Roy's employees. They have to stay in a toxic and demoralizing culture just to survive. Because so many people can only afford to live paycheck to paycheck, simply walking away from an abusive workplace culture is simply not feasible anymore. Walking away means the lights don't get turned on, gas doesn't get put in the car, and the kids don't eat. And companies know this is reality for most of their workforce. They use this knowledge as leverage to do whatever they want to their dedicated teams of employees. It is sad on so many levels. They can treat them however they want because they know they need a job. It will be incredibly hard on them to find another. So, the thinking is that it is better to stay in a horrible job than to not have one at all.

Treat your employees like they matter. Demoralizing them does not generate productivity. Dehumanizing does not bring better performance. If employees are made to feel like second-best, that is how they will treat your customers.

Perks vs. Culture

There is a major disconnect in the corporate world whereby organizations think company perks are the same as company culture. But ping-pong tables, gourmet meals and casual dress down days do not define company culture. Rather, it is the behavior tolerated that sets the precedent. A culture can be filled with total jerks who wear jeans on Friday. A ping-pong table does not stop a micromanager from being abusive and overbearing. Free lunches on Friday don't promote a productive environment. Yes, these are all very nice perks to attract potential candidates, but they do not constitute the integral components of a successful company culture.

I read a post on the employment social networking site LinkedIn that says it best:

> Years ago, I quit my job. My boss texted me a day later and asked me to come back. He said, 'What happened?' and I said, 'Nothing happened'. He then went on to say, 'If nothing happened, then why can't you come back?' I responded that the reason I quit was just for that reason...*nothing happened*. Never a lunch, coffee, or a simple acknowledgement of landing a massive account. *Nothing*.[2]

It is important for companies to remember that when an employee has lost all hope in their workplace culture, the damage is often irreversible. They will seek out a company who is of higher character and treats them like family. Nothing is more disheartening for a person than going to a job they are not welcome at.

It is amazing how corporate executives and human resource managers will sit and scratch their heads as to why they cannot retain good people. Would you work for yourself based on how you treat others? If you had a supervisor or manager who treated you the way you treat others, would you want to give it your all for that company?

I once applied to a local financial institution who threatened to call the police on me. My crime? I called their human resources representative to ask for an update on my application. I had not heard anything back for several months, and wanted a simple update. To this day, this bank has not been able to fill positions. They have numerous postings on job boards and websites. No one wants to work there, and I can see why. When you treat people badly, word will get around and no one will want to work with you.

Corporate executives don't need to sit back and be perplexed; they already know the answer. Treat people with respect. If you are generous to your employees, they will want to stay longer and work harder. If you kick out the jerks, the team will respond with positive productivity.

I read the comments of one of the worst reviewed companies in the state of Utah on a job placement website. Consistently, employees reveal a company culture that treats front line staff as nothing more than a workaholic machines while management places friends and family in higher senior positions. This has caused severe team demoralization. Employees complain of being fired on the spot for simply asking for help or additional training on a certain issue. The most consistent comment on these reviewers was the same: "I never felt valued." Strangely, I found the only common factor these employees seemed to like was the free lunch on Fridays.

There is a story being told here. Generally, when I see one negative review, I dismiss it. I might take a little more interest if there are three or four bad reviews. But at the time of this writing, there were eighty-nine reviews, all telling the same story. Something bad is happening at this organization, and a free lunch is not the solution. There is a genuine disconnect. There is favoritism. There is a genuine lack of empathy.

In This Together

Every religion in the world has a teaching pertaining to being part of the greater human family. We may look, act and talk different, but in the end, it is our common humanity that binds us together as people. Many religions teach that we are the products of a mighty Creator, that we share a divine ancestry and origin. Now, I am not advocating bringing religious teachings into the workplace, so please don't read too far into this. I am also not suggesting that the workplace be a therapy session or place to solve our emotional issues. In the end, a business is there to make money, and employees are paid to do a job. But what must happen in the workplace is a spirit of humanity. Kindness, empathy, compassion and decency are required, no matter where we go or what we do in this life.

One of the most basic elements of humanity is communication with one another. When we ask a question, we expect an answer. When we are not given one, we are flooded with feelings of doubt and confusion. This is especially true within human resources. One of the biggest frustrations I have is when human resource professionals fail to show even the most basic effort to communicate to candidates. I feel it is unprofessional and outright rude. It sends a very strong signal that a company does not view them as human, that there is not a real person sitting on the other end of the computer filling out an application or resume. It tells a candidate that they are not important enough to even warrant a basic response, that they are sub-human and are not entitled to a basic courtesy.

I have told you a lot about my human resources manager friend who works for the fastest growing city in Utah. We often share our thoughts about how disconnected human resources has become. On this issue of responding to candidates, he shared with me that from 2018-2019, over 500 candidates applied for city jobs and never received a basic email confirming their application was received. He told me that this was unacceptable, and he instructed his staff to make phone calls to every applicant and apologize. It was a lot of work, but he knew it was the right thing to do. For him, investing in people brings a far better return on investment than making money.

He shared with me another story involving one of his employees who was experiencing some very tough times emotionally. He asked the city if he could bring an emotional support animal to work. My friend explained that the only animals allowed in city buildings were service animals approved by the Americans with Disabilities Act. While the employee was upset, my friend took extra time to meet with him privately and offer support. Because of this, he was able to see a doctor and got additional help. That employee is now in a better emotional position and is performing better at his job. The employee also has a new respect for his manager and his city. A new level of trust, communication and understanding was obtained by all involved. I have incredible respect for him and his efforts to bring basic humanity into the workplace. He demonstrates that a little act of kindness can go a long way and that he is committed to treating people right.

I find great strength in the saying, "When we lift one another, we rise stronger together." When you see someone struggling at work, offer to step in and help them. Look out for them and show concern for their personal struggles. Ask them what you can do to help. You may not be able to help with all their needs, but you can build them up so one day they can be there for another person in need. You can become their friend, their ally and supporter. You can take them out to dinner or help clean their house on a day off, or just do something to show you care. You stand with them, beside them, and with them. This is not an easy thing to do and won't work with every person. Some people are naturally rude and have deep emotional issues that can only be helped by competent professionals. Some are addicted to narcotics and need additional help. You are not required to make others happy. You should put your needs and the needs of your family first. But you are asked to be kind and to be of service. If a person does not want your help, then you have made a valiant effort to lend a hand. But if you try to please everyone, it will lead to incredible confusion, frustration, and misery for all parties involved. But we can all be kind. We can all strive to be good people. We can offer to be of service. That costs us absolutely *nothing,* and the reward is often greater than we ever expected.

Fired for Doing Good

I read a horrific story involving a company who fired an employee for going above and beyond for a customer. On Christmas Eve of 2019, US Bank employee Emily James received a call from a distraught customer named Marc Euginio. He was concerned because a computer error placed his paycheck on hold from his employer, leaving him broke. He attempted to reach out to his local branch office but was left without any results since all offices had closed early for the holiday. He contacted the national call center and was begging for help. He was at a local gas station and needed twenty dollars to get home. Emily sprang into action. Rarely would she get a call from someone local, but felt this was a unique opportunity to take accountability for a problem caused by her employer. She obtained permission from a supervisor to leave and drove a few miles to the customer. She handed him money out of her wallet, said "Merry Christmas", and promptly returned to work. On New Year's Eve, she was informed she was being terminated on the grounds of "improper interaction with a customer."

US Bank issued a statement reading:

> "At US Bank, we have policies and procedures in place to protect our customers and employees. Ms. James was terminated following an internal investigation into her interactions with a customer. During this review it was determined Ms. James did not use the available

solutions to remedy the customer's situation and instead put herself and the bank at risk with her actions."[3]

I personally believe this woman is a saint, and this story demonstrates how destructive business has become. It is tragic how companies have taken all the humanity out of the business world and have instituted policies that only favor the bottom line. What risk was taken? There were no options available. Had she lifted the hold on the check, she would have been fired. The local branch office was closed, and the manager was the only one who could override the computer. What choice was left? The company made a clear mistake and took no accountability for the issue. They did not care it was Christmas Eve and the customer was stranded due to their mistake. This man was trying to see his children and spend a special time of year with them; this meant nothing to the bank. They did not view this man as a human, but rather as just another statistic who kept the salaries of the senior executives coming. This woman showed good judgement and moral character to remedy a situation that was caused not directly by her, but by the company she worked for. She made a situation better for a customer. This woman deserves a promotion, not a termination. It is, frankly, an asinine demonstration of corporate culture at its worst. Many companies tout how they care about customers. But their so-called commitment is nothing more than a propaganda slogan. Their mission statement is void of all substance and meaning. Upon reading this, my heart broke for this woman. If I had the power to hire her, I would. She obviously has a service mindset. She recognizes that being a decent person in business is more important than making money. In this case, US Bank did everything wrong to promote a positive employee and customer service driven culture. Now, employees will probably be more scared to do the right thing for people due to a fear of losing their jobs, which will impact the customer experience in a negative way.

Bottom Line: Maribeth Bisinere, Senior Vice President for Walt Disney World Theme Parks, states:

> "It [an exceptional customer experience] requires people, but more importantly, it requires people who care. When you develop an entire population of employees who care and are empowered to create memories for guests, continually exceeding customer expectation is buying into your culture"[4]

President John F. Kennedy summed it up best. "Our most basic common link is that we all inhabit this small planet. We all breathe the same air. We all cherish our children's future. And we are all mortal."[5]

We all have dreams and hopes. We all have fears. We all struggle with real and sometimes debilitating issues. Why should I work well for someone when all they do is make me feel bad? I have enough bad things to deal with in my personal life; my workplace should not be one of them. Why should I bring profit to a company who treats me as a number rather than a person? When you treat people right, they will want to produce results for you. They will want to make you money. They will want to treat customers better. This leads to a better experience for your customer and thus better profit for you. The world is barren, quickly being drained of decency and hope. With so much hate, with so much meaningless division, and people pitted against people for no good reason, it is crucial now more than ever to extend the basic human kindness to employees, to candidates, and to one another. Doing so reaps the rewards of better profits. But don't do it for profit; do it because it's the *right* thing to do.

Chapter 4
Happy Employees, Happy Sales

"The way management treats associates is exactly how associates will treat customers" – Sam Walton

IN 2015, *STAR Wars: The Force Awakens* featured the Starkiller Base, a planet converted into a superweapon that could destroy an entire world millions of miles away with one shot.

When I think of some work cultures, this image is the first one that comes to mind. Rather than a star killer, there are some corporate cultures that are *soul* killers. They are as destructive to the person as the fictional weapon in the movie. They can take all the motivation, energy, drive, and ambition out of you. Negative workplace cultures can leave you with feelings of anxiety, dread, and even fear. Richard Branson said it best: "There is no magic formula for great company culture. The key is just treating your staff how you would want to be treated"[1] So simple, yet sadly this is a lost concept among many of today's corporate cultures.

There are numerous articles and curricula out there about what creates a positive and productive corporate culture. I will leave the expert and in-depth opinions to others. I will simply convey what I have found to be successful through my own experiences of being both a manager and a direct report.

- **Lack of micromanaging/autonomy:** I think we can all agree that micromanaging is the number one destroyer of workplace cultures. Micromanaging is a fancy way of saying, "I don't trust you and need to control you." We as human beings were never meant to be controlled. We are independent, free-thinking beings with incredible capability and potential. If given the tools, we can do the job. Micromanagers, however, are just the opposite. You know how most computer applications have an actual "print" button at the top of the screen? You know how most computer programs will let you also print something by right-clicking? A micromanager will tell you that you *have* to print something one particular way and no other (yes, I have *actually* experienced this!). They fail to see that there are multiple ways to accomplishing the same task because it interferes with the flow of their perfect world. It's very similar to the movie *GI Jane*. Master Chief Urgayle (brilliantly played by Vigo Mortensen) is the drill instructor in charge of turning rough recruits into Navy Seals. To show his true authority, he proclaims in a soft voice, "The ebb and flow of the Atlantic tides, the drift of the continents, the very position of the sun along its ecliptic. These are just a *few* of the things I control in my world." A great movie quote but a sad illustration of the level of control in many corporate cultures. Micromanagers thus create a loss of trust among employees. But the table turns both ways. If you don't trust me, then why should I trust you? Employees see a micromanager as a robot, someone void of human feeling who has created an unnecessary barrier blocking communication and productivity. Micromanagers also have a genuine fear of failure. According to the *Harvard Business Review*, the suspect cause of micromanaging is a fear-driven mechanism with pride at its source.[2] Yes, everyone should strive to set goals and meet them. But I can also tell you from firsthand experience that failure is a *positive* thing! Most mistakes can be fixed, most negative situations reversed and turned into positives, and most defeats turned into triumphs. I have failed many times as a leader and a manager. But in life, the greatest successes are often rooted in the deepest failures. Comedian Conan O'Brien said it best:

> It is our failures ... that define us and make us unique. It's not easy, but if you accept misfortune and handle it right, your perceived failures can become a catalyst for profound reinvention.[3]

- **Empowerment:** Just the opposite of micromanaging is empowerment. It is giving your employees the tools and resources to do the job on their own with little oversight from a manager. It is saying to them, "I trust you to do the right thing," and often that trust is found to be deserved rather than misplaced. A company that exhibits this the best (in my humble opinion) is my go-to company, the Ritz-Carlton. Known for setting the gold standard in not only customer service but corporate development, Ritz-Carlton developed a program that allows every employee, from the housekeeper to the CEO, to have a $2,000 line of credit that can be used at any time to make a guest happy.[4] No management approval, no committees or paperwork. Just an element of trust that the money is being used to improve the guest experience. Now talk about empowerment! The stories of how this has not only improved the overall guest experience but employee morale at Ritz-Carlton are far too numerous to mention here. But the point I want to drive home is that enabling your employees to make decisions on their own gives them a greater sense of pride in their work. Now they can look at a completed task and with confidence say, "Yeah, I did that!"

- **Performance and praise**: Not to belabor the point, but human beings need to feel valued and that they have a purpose. They need to know they are welcome, appreciated, and needed. As a manager, I strive to commend my employees every chance I can when they do something positive. It can be something as small as grabbing them a candy bar from the snack machine or buying them their favorite soft drink. A practice I became pretty religious about doing was taking down notes with my new hires, documenting their favorite drink, candy bar, snack food, and restaurant. I would then pull out that list from their file when I wanted to recognize them for a job well done. Any Joe Schmo can order a plaque online and set it on someone's desk every quarter. Rather, the old saying of "it's the thought that counts" is what prevails here. My employees would tell me that the ninety-nine-cent bottle of their favorite drink meant more to them than some meaningless plaque ordered by some executive assistant who has used the same font and text for the last ten years. I have seen employees cry when I recognized they were trying hard and gave them a genuine "Job well done."

- **Work/life balance:** Ah-ha, the glue that holds it all together! Companies that recognize that their employees are in fact people with real lives outside of work find those same employees are more productive and happier while at work. Tony Hsieh, CEO of Zappos, was asked about this very topic.

  > There are companies that focus on work-life separation or work-life balance and at Zappos we really focus on work-life integration and at the end of the day it's just life … and especially if you spend so much time at work you better enjoy the time that you're spending there and people that you're with.[5]

  Hsieh expounds further:

  > We want the person to be the same person at home or in the office because what we've found is that's when the great ideas come out, that's when their creativity shines. When people are in that environment, that's when the passion comes out and that's really what's driven a lot of our growth over the years.[6]

  There is a beautiful country song that illustrates this point. *The Dollar* is written from the perspective of a little boy who wants to spend some time with his father, but he must go to work. The little boy asks his mother where his daddy goes each day, and the mother explains that daddy is paid for his time. The little boy rushes and grabs fifty-five cents from his piggy bank and asks his mother how much time that will buy him with his dad. With tears in his eyes, he tells his mother if he needs more, he has some leftover tooth-fairy money. The song is, to say the least, a tear-jerker, but really emphasizes this issue. Employees need time away from work. They need to pursue their dreams and their passions. A healthy work/life balance must be negotiated at every organization.

- **Engagement:** Science has shown us that the best barometer of a company's culture is the engagement of its employees. Strong cultures are filled with active and productive employees, while negative ones are filled with disengaged individuals and high turnover rates. David Brown of Deloitte & Touche stated the following:

    > Engagement and culture can become a competitive advantage or an Achilles heel. Culture and engagement are now serious business issues, not just topics for HR to debate. And in this world of glass door transparency and social media, companies have nowhere to hide![7]

The Society for Human Resource Managers reported companies with engaged workforces demonstrated a 19 percent higher operating income, compared to 34 percent less operating income by those companies that do not have an engaged culture.[8] Employee engagement is what drives people to be their best. At the front of this book is a picture I drew in my spare time. It is a burned-out, overworked man sitting in front of his computer. He is a representation of employees who work at organizations that fail to foster any of the topics I have spoken about thus far. They are paycheck-collecting chair warmers. They come to work, do their assigned jobs, and leave. It is not their fault; rather, it is all they know. They have not been empowered, developed, or rewarded. No wonder they lack the most basic customer-service skills. There is a 1996 episode of the television series *Roseanne* that really drives home this point. David moves out of the Conner house and takes a job at a strange theme park in Lanford, Illinois. He is transformed into an eerily smiling automation. Every day, he and his fellow co-workers have a dedicated time to practice smiling and being perky. He is forced to use dedicated scripts and phrases on park guests. Then, in a cult like fashion, he is lined up to recite the company motto five times a day as a morale booster. He loses all sense of his identity and becomes a witless servant of the megacorporation. The episode was a humorous jab at the Walt Disney Company acquiring the American Broadcasting Company (ABC) and was meant to be in good fun. But it really paints a picture of how a lack of positive employee engagement can break an organization. Reciting mottos and mission statements does not foster engagement. Mindless and pre-scripted lingo does not cultivate a spirit of creativity; engagement fosters engagement!

- **Cultural reinforcement:** Every business has an employee or set of employees who are what I call the "best jerks on the planet." They are great at what they do but have a horrible attitude while doing it. They can close sales like it's nothing to them. They bring in the big bucks. But they are condescending and rude and can poison whatever good fruit is being produced. I had to work with someone like this. This individual wore many hats as an office manager, accountant, and human resources manager. This person is still working at the same company to this day. I know this person is well organized and can multitask like no other. Sadly, this person is also an incredibly toxic person to be around. She has a boorish and condescending personality. She makes other employees feel completely unwelcome. I can honestly say that I am usually never in favor of terminating someone if I can avoid it. After all, it is a loss of income for that person, and their world will be turned upside down. But I did say *usually*. In this particular case, and in a few select others, toxic individuals who pollute a company workplace are dangerous to the organization and need to be removed. Tony Hsieh states the following:

> Even if a person is great at their job, even if they're a superstar at their job, if they're bad for our culture, we'll fire them for that reason alone.[9]

Isador Sharp, founder of the world-famous Four Seasons Resorts and Hotels, speaks to this point with more eloquence and class than I ever could:

> We put in place a commitment to the Golden Rule: treating people with the respect and dignity they are entitled to ... was it difficult? Absolutely! We had people at the very senior level of this company who wouldn't abide by it, so I was personally having a very difficult time because I knew that if these senior employees weren't

going to walk the walk, we would have to separate them from the company. And that is exactly what we did. Many senior executives were terminated because they would give our values lip service rather than sincere attention.[10]

To sum it up, the culture that prevails at an organization is the one that is *allowed*

The Bill Lumbergh School of Management

One of the best movies ever made was the 1999 cult classic *Office Space* with Ron Livingston and Gary Cole. Livingston portrays Peter Gibbons, an overstressed and underappreciated employee who feels zero satisfaction from his work and his life. His boss, Bill Lumbergh (Cole), is the embodiment of an ineffective micromanager. Bill will often sneak up on unsuspecting employees about to leave work for the day (and often on a Friday) and inform them they are being called into work despite having already made weekend plans. Then, in a sarcastic tone, Lumbergh will thank the employee for their "cooperation" in doing so.

In the middle of the movie, Gibbons is summoned to a meeting with two consultants (coincidently both named Bob) that have been hired by his large, cultureless company in an effort to boost morale and production. He confesses to them that his only real motivation for coming to work is his fear of losing his job, reminding them that that kind of company culture will only cause a person to work just barely hard enough not to get fired.

I believe this movie was way ahead of its time. It was a precursor to *The Office*, but this movie embodies the mundane, ordinary, and joyless work cultures that exist in the world and how people's sole motivation for working is collecting a paycheck. Now this movie is incredibly vulgar and offensive at times, so it is not for every person out there. But it makes a valid point. A person should never lower and devalue themselves for money. Working in a toxic culture with toxic people who see you as a means to an end is truly a soul-killing experience. No one deserves that.

I remember an experience where I had to work with a Bill Lumbergh type of individual. As a senior finance director for a large auto dealership, I worked with a sales manager who was Bill Lumbergh in real life. He saw everyone as car-selling machines that only needed to be greased and oiled regularly to continue working. His attitude was smug, and he never admitted his faults. He believed the bottom line was more crucial than the happiness of individuals. This dealership had posted hours (earlier than most), with an early closing time on Saturdays. I am sure I speak for the many hardworking auto professionals out there when I say that after working extensive overtime, late into the evening, day in and day out, one looks forward to an early night away from work with friends and family. But not this manager! On a certain Saturday night, it was three minutes before closing. Suddenly, out of nowhere, two potential customers walked in. They said they were interested in purchasing a car. Despite posted business hours, all banks being closed, and having exhausted employees, this manager proceeded to begin the car-buying process, which on average takes a minimum of two hours. The customers asked if they should come back on Monday, to which the sales manager responded, "It's not like these guys have anything going on! They are happy to stay!" Just like that, we were labeled as expendable, lifeless drones who did not need a break. To this organization, employees are treated on the same level as the Borg from *Star Trek*.

With that, right then and there, I decided I would cease my employment with that organization. Yes, I was making very good money. But working in a toxic and soul-killing culture for the sake of a paycheck is no different than Judas selling out for thirty pieces of silver. Yes, I do believe that the customer's needs should be served, but there were other ways that could have been handled.

An employee-focused manager would have said something like this in lieu of what was actually said: "Mr. Customer, I really do appreciate you coming in to purchase a car from us! We know you have a lot of choices, and I thank you for choosing us. But my guys have been working very hard this week, and we are a few minutes away from our posted closing time. They need to be with their families. Could I get your information, and on Monday, we can make something happen first thing in the morning?"

Another option would be asking an employee if they would be willing to stay afterhours. I am confident that a salesman would have agreed to get a test drive going, had they been asked. It was being treated like foot soldiers in the moneymaking army, with no purpose but to respond to the commands of the general that was not appropriate for me. Behavior like this is a culture crusher, a giant Godzilla-like creature that destroys everything and everyone in its wake. Employees know when they are being taken advantage of. Employees know when they are not welcome or valued. And they will leave in a mass exodus that will rival the biblical one.

Bryan Horn

We're Just Employees

As a bank manager, I spent several hours cleaning the back offices of the branch, a place that only a select few would see. I spent less time on the front because I knew that a janitorial company would clean up several times a week, and we as employees would maintain a proper front of house for customers in between. But in this case, the back had been neglected, with disorganized papers everywhere, dust, and a musty smell. After spending hours cleaning, an employee came up to me and genuinely looked confused. "Why are you cleaning? It's just us back here!"

With that statement, I learned a valuable lesson. I learned that I had not done enough to show my employees how much I appreciated them and valued them. I felt horrible that this employee thought of herself using the word *just*, as if they were *just* employees who don't matter. I tend to think a lot of managers and businesses see their employees as *just* that, a means to an end. "That's *just* a garbage man" or "That's *just* the janitor." I made it a point to correct that employee. I reinforced my belief that the bank employees, from tellers to loan officers, were every bit as crucial and valuable as I was. They were not *just* employees, but they were valued partners in the success of my branch. At least, that is how I tried to treat them. I wanted the back office to be just as nice as the front (or as close as possible) so that in some small way, my employees felt welcomed. Everyone deserves a place to relax, unwind, and forget about their job, if only for an hour. That space should be inviting and welcoming, just like the front of the house is for the customers. So, I dusted and mopped. I organized all the bank paperwork and put it into file drawers. I bought a TV and a DVD player with some movies to watch. I even donated my old Nintendo playing system for employees to use during break times. I would buy flowers or even just a nice-smelling diffuser to make things smell a little better. I did what I could, and I noticed my employees reacted with a sense of greater self-esteem when they returned from the back office.

One day, I was sick in bed with a cold, so of course I turned on my phone and went straight to YouTube to binge-watch pointless videos. I came across a video that I thought would be entertaining but turned out to also be eye-opening on this very topic.

This video from 2016 was an insight into the life of the executive chef on a Royal Caribbean cruise ship. Now, I will not even attempt to define how amazing it is to see a team of two hundred chefs prepare ten thousand meals a day, take a one-hour break, and do it all over again. I can't begin to explain how many principles of leadership, management, and teamwork can be extracted from this one video alone. You can easily search this out on your own and take from it your own insights. What I want to point out is the dedication to the crew morale by setting a backstage that rivals the front of house. In this video, the executive chef proudly shares that he has more than twenty-seven nationalities represented in his various kitchens, and there are more than 112 nationalities among the entire crew. He explains how his chefs try to represent as many of those nationalities as possible in the food choices provided in the crew cafeteria. And we are not talking about ramen noodles and store-bought sushi being served. The same level of preparation and service that goes into preparing meals for the passengers is done for the crew. The crew cafeteria has a wide selection of beverages, entrees, and desserts to savor. There are comfortable chairs and well-prepared tables, just like in the fancy ballrooms and restaurants on the passenger decks. There are linen napkins instead of paper ones. There is also a dedicated karaoke lounge, bar, video arcade, and pool/spa for crew use. It is apparent that Royal Caribbean gets it. They understand the importance of setting the stage for their staff as equal or close to that of the guests. They truly know that these thousands of crew members who perform every function of a floating city are vital to the operation of the ship. It is a place they will be living for most of their professional lives, so why not make it as close to home as possible? What I took away most from this video was, believe it or not, the napkins. Sure, it would be much more affordable to use paper napkins. But linen invokes just an extra touch of class, saying to that crew member, "You are every bit as important as a passenger. You deserve a touch of class too!"

The Best Coach Is Also the Water Boy

In the banking world, the entry level position is that of a teller. It is one of the most underappreciated jobs in any industry, which is why there is such a high turnover of tellers in banking. That poor person must deal with bad attitudes and complex customer problems, be responsible for their money, remember countless policies and procedures, get yelled at, and do it all while keeping a smile. I truly admire and commend these banking professionals, and it was always a genuine pleasure to promote these talented individuals.

Some managers are like the guys on the Roman ships who would yell, "Row! Row! Row!" to the unfortunate prisoners of war who were about to be enslaved. A manager who sits and yells all day to make things go faster does not build leadership or respect. Rather, they build resentment and hostility. As an employee, why should I work faster and harder when I won't even get a thank you for it anyway?

I held the position of a traveling support bank manager. In short, I covered twenty-four different branches of a large western bank when the manager on duty was away at a meeting, or on vacation, or was not able to be in the office that day. Sometimes my branch assignments would last a day, and some would last months. I recall going to a branch where the only concern of the manager was planning her next vacation rather than motivating her employees. She would rarely grant vacation time to her direct reports but would brag about how long of a vacation she would be taking. She would consistently hash out orders for the tellers to move faster while sitting in her office looking up vacation packages and flights. Putting it bluntly, this manager was very bad at being a manager. I covered this branch for a couple of days and did what I thought were normal manager duties. I would commend the tellers if they handled a difficult situation professionally. I would pull a teller drawer and run transactions when I could see them getting overworked and overwhelmed. My doing this caused confusion among them, and they were not afraid to tell me why. They were so used to being treated as *just* tellers and not as valued employees that they didn't know what to make of my being nice to them. They told me that the manager never pulled a teller drawer during busy times. She never complimented them, so they were made to feel as if they were not worthy of praise. I remember thinking about how tragic and sad it was for these dedicated professionals to be treated this way. An effective manager is one who will coach the team but will also be the water boy. They will get down and dirty and do the jobs they think they are above. Not only does this produce confidence and respect, but it promotes humility within yourself. I truly believe that the big executives who make decisions do so because they don't do the very jobs they assign others to do. Maybe they would think twice about the policies and procedures they enact for those frontline employees if they did.

Bottom Line: Now more than ever, it is crucial for companies to invest in their employees and see them as valued, essential and wanted partners for the successful operation of a business. Engagement, work-life balance, performance, praise, and empowerment are just some of the many tools in the building of a successful corporate culture. Every organization is different. Your organization may have a vastly different budget than another. Treating employees as valued partners rather than moneymaking seat warmers does not cost you one red cent but can yield productive results. Engaged employees produce outstanding service, which generates brand loyalty and increased sales. This is not a complex formula for success. It really is that simple. Use your best judgment, and maybe even some employee insight, to make this happen!

Chapter 5
Setting the Stage

"All the world is a stage" – William Shakespeare

WHEN I WAS EIGHT years old, I had the rare opportunity to see the original cast of *The Phantom of the Opera* in Los Angeles, with the legendary Michael Crawford as the Phantom. I still vividly recall the experience, so much so that some thirty years later, I still have the original program and ticket stub from the performance. I remember the ornate lobby of Ahmanson Theater and the little booths set up selling Phantom memorabilia such as T-shirts, coffee mugs, and cassette tape (yes, you heard me right) soundtracks. I remember being dressed up in a tuxedo, as it was a black-tie performance. I remember walking into a dimly lit theater with a massive stage and thousands of seats made to resemble the Paris Opera in the late 1890s. Dark, deep red curtains flanked with ornate gold statues were front and center. As patrons flowed into the theater, there was almost a reverence about what was to be experienced. I remember looking around in every direction, taking in the majesty of the theater. And then the lights went dark, the curtain came up, and the production began. For those of you who have never seen this amazing production, you might want to stop reading this part, for there is about to be a spoiler! The prologue of the show begins some twenty-five years after the story ends, with an auctioneer selling off items from the vault of the opera house. On the stage is a massive brown tarp covering a destroyed chandelier. To this day, I get goose bumps thinking about how amazing it was to hear the auctioneer saying, "Perhaps we may frighten away the ghost of so many years ago, with a little illumination ..." And then *boom!* A ball of fire and smoke rise from the brown covering as the iconic organ theme begins to play. The chandelier rises from the ashes and reassembles itself in midair as theater patrons watch the Paris Opera House come alive. It is truly one of the most spectacular moments in musical theater, and I have yet to find a production that tops that single moment.

What does it take to put on a production such as this one?

- The chandelier alone has more than six thousand beads, weighs more than two thousand pounds, and is three meters wide.
- It takes more than two hours to put on the Phantom's makeup, including prosthetics, two wigs, two radio microphones, and contact lenses.
- Each performance has 230 costume changes, 14 dressers, 120 automated cues, 22 scene changes, and 130 cast, crew, and orchestra members.[1]

To accomplish such an elaborate production requires an equally talented and dedicated cast of people. In an organization that puts on this type of production, every member of the cast is critical. And what happens in the back of house is vital to the front-of-house production being successful.

I use this example to set the stage as to how important it is to set the stage (yes, ironic pun intended). This chapter will focus on the little things that make an organization successful, the "quiet whispers," as the Disney Institute calls them, that make or break a customer's perception and how to raise the bar at each customer interaction.[2]

Perception of the Production

In 1995, the late Robin Williams starred in the movie *Jumanji* about a boy who gets trapped inside a board game. Everything within the game becomes real life. For example, his small town turns into a jungle, wild elephants roam the streets, and so forth. There is a scene in which Williams and the cast are evading a dangerous hunter. They run into a department store called Sir Save-a-Lot, which had the slogan "The customer is king!" posted above every aisle.

Meaningless catch phrases such as these are outdated attempts by organizations to give the illusion they are paying attention to customers. However, the experience delivered to customers tells them they are not kings or queens, but rather are lowly subjects who serve the needs of the master. Understanding the perceptions of the customer is crucial to setting the stage. If you don't know you're your customer wants, how can you cater to them? If the customer does not *feel* like they are on the receiving end of great service, then it is a worthless endeavor. According to a 2017 research study, "More than two-thirds of marketers responsible say their companies compete mostly on the basis of customer experience. In two years' time, 81%

say they expect to be competing mostly or completely on the basis of customer experience.³

Sadly, many company executives have enacted policies where decision making is too far removed from the very people who are dealing with a customer and yet the customer facing staff is expected to deliver the best service experience at the point of sale. The saying goes, "You can't have your cake and eat it too." A company cannot reasonably expect its team to deliver world class service if they don't empower them to do so! It really is not a complicated formula, rather just common sense.

Every Cast Member Deserves Applause

At the conclusion of a musical theatre production, the entire cast will return on stage for a curtain call. This is an opportunity for the audience to show their appreciation in the form of applause for what they have just seen. Every cast member gets a moment to be recognized. The cast will then gesture to the orchestra members and the backstage crew, acknowledging those behind the scenes. Every person in the cast made that show possible, and all equally deserves to be recognized.

Disney has always held the belief that an organization is a theater production, and every person in the cast is equally crucial. If the guy who pulled the curtain wasn't important, then you would never see the show! If the girl who set the costumes out wasn't important, the entire cast would be on stage in street clothes.

There is a wonderful story about a janitor who worked for NASA. President John F. Kennedy was visiting the Johnson Space Center in 1962 when he noticed a janitor carrying a broom. The president stopped the tour with high-ranking space agency officials to speak with the man.

"Hi, I'm Jack Kennedy. What are you doing?"

"Well, Mr. President," the janitor responded, "I'm helping to put a man on the moon!"[4]

There is great power in this story. Many corporate cultures would view this man as *just* a janitor. But he knew his true worth, that he was part of a larger story being told. If every company on the planet embraced this belief, the world would be a better place to work in.

I remember going to a business where I had the misfortune of hearing how a manager talked to an employee behind the scenes. This guy was so loud that you could clearly hear every word he said through his thick office door. He was ripping apart some young new employee. The manager and the employee emerged, one in tears and the other with a big smile. I am sure you can figure out which one was which. The manager approached me and acted as if nothing had just transpired and proceeded to talk to me like I was his best friend.

This really put me at odds. So, I committed right then and there to always treat my employees the same as my customers. Ritz-Carlton reinforces this principle:

> The message has to be the same everywhere. If I am only hospitable with my guests, then it's not three-dimensional anymore. Let's say you are in the hospitality business, but you wouldn't give a great room to one of your employees staying in your own hotel. Examples like this happen all the time, and it gets very confusing to employees.[5]

Steve Bartolin, chairman of the Broadmoor Hotel, expresses a similar thought: "Our approach is that we are all in this together. We treat everyone with dignity and respect, no matter your job title."[6] At the risk of sounding like a broken record, I cannot stress enough how important it is to create a culture of service among your employees. But setting the stage does not stop at how you talk to your employees. Oh no! It simply *begins* there.

Appearances Matter

People need all five senses to operate, and they often use them to decide something. This is especially true when we make decisions about where to spend our money. When we think of a loved one out of state, we try to envision what that person might enjoy as we browse aisle upon aisle in a store. We literally can smell the store we are shopping in and can envision the smell of the products in our own homes. Why do you think new-car smell is not only the most popular fabric scent on the market but is one of the number one reasons customers want a new car?

Think of how important the power of sight alone is. Of all the senses, it is the main one we use to make a decision. How we look at things not only helps us make a split-second decision about if we want it, but it will determine the experience from beginning to end.

Imagine going to a fast-food restaurant compared to that of a fine-dining establishment. At a fast-food restaurant, you are likely going to find reheated food slobbered with some random condiment, then hastily half wrapped in a piece of colorful paper and thrown onto a dirty tray. I can speak from countless experiences of opening the sandwich and thinking to myself, *This is the ugliest-looking thing I have ever seen!* Even though we know that the presentation does not necessarily affect the taste, it still does something to us mentally. We taste by seeing.

Let's transition now and imagine walking into a five-star restaurant. As you enter, a host will warmly welcome you to the establishment, personally escort you to a table, slide your chair back, and gesture for you to sit down. You will have a sensory overload. The smell of delicious food cooking in the kitchen and the sight of clean tables and well-dressed staff will almost be too much to handle. Then you will feel the fine linens and tableware. Finally, there is the presentation of the food. It is almost a work of art, something you want to frame and take home with you.

Eating at a place like this is not just a means to an end; it truly is an experience to be remembered. Like my one time visiting The Plaza, it is an experience of a lifetime. Take the world-famous The Inn at Little Washington, Patrick O'Connell's double-five-star restaurant and hotel (from Forbes and AAA) in the remote town of Rappahannock, Virginia. It is a destination experience, being "30 minutes past the middle of nowhere."[7] Despite its rural location, it has hosted heads of state, politicians, and celebrities. But it also has catered to the average person who saves up for quite some time to take their special someone for a luxurious dining experience. O'Connell is a master when it comes to providing the warmest, most welcoming experience possible. These are his words:

> We focus completely and totally on one person, even if only for a matter of seconds, yet long enough that you've got a clear connection, a channel between the two of you. It's the ability to focus so intensely on a guest that the rest of the world ceases to exist.[8]

Micah Solomon notes that the success of this restaurant has many contributing factors, such as the training of the kitchen staff, the décor by London stage designer Joyce Evans, and exclusive farm-to-table food sourcing. Think for a moment how important appearances are for a place that is literally out in the middle of nowhere and has attracted some of the most powerful people in the world to its dinner table. That fact alone tells you what kind of service is to be expected when you walk through the doors.

Am I the only one who is disappointed at how the hamburger looks on the menu compared to how it actually comes out on the tray? Why do fast-food companies spend millions of dollars a year paying professional food photographers to make their latest burger look as appetizing as possible? I think it is because these companies know the power of appearances. I just wish they enforced those standards at the prep counter.

The delivery system of your product or service is an equal contributing factor to the sale of your product or service. How you present it and the environment around it is as crucial as the actual features. Remember, you're not just selling something; you are selling an experience. Put your best foot forward, bring it all together, and let it shine!

Everything Speaks

I was watching the movie *Shrek* with a family member on a brand-new high-definition television that he had just purchased. He was shocked at how clear the picture was. I remember him saying, "You can even see the reflection in the water!" as Shrek walked by. That got me thinking about the little things that make up an experience, the quiet whispers I mentioned in this chapter that you may never have seen, heard, or known about but that contribute to the overall experience.

Using *Shrek* as a baseline for this, I began researching little-known facts about the movie. For example, in Shrek's face alone, there are more than 180 animations to control everything from an eyebrow to his smile. More than 1,250 props and various environments with thirty-six unique locations were featured, more than any other computer-animated film. There are more than 28,186 trees, with more than three billion leaves throughout the film. There are more than 1,500 individual people with distinct characteristics in the cathedral wedding scene. The list of little details goes on and on.[9]

When you step back and examine these facts, it really is a testament to the power of the stage, to the little things and quiet whispers that make something magical. I know that I could watch *Shrek* a million times over and probably never catch all the little details. But I also know that if one of those 28,186 trees were missing, it would take something away from the entire production. I love how Disney drives home this point: "The importance of managing the effect of setting on the guest experience can be summed up in two words: *everything speaks*."[10]

Everything from the cleanliness of the building to the greeting given as customers walk in your doors speaks volumes as to what the customer is going to experience.

Let's look at the call center experience I had with a major American discount airliner. I was planning a short trip from Utah to Arizona for Memorial Day weekend. Instead of traveling an hour to Salt Lake International and flying a more well-known national carrier, I decided to go thrifty and use the budget airline that flew out of the smaller Provo Regional Airport, which is only ten minutes away. Well, I soon found out that the old saying of "you get what you pay for" was very true. I was on hold for more than thirty minutes. Once finally connected, an agent provided as little information as possible, referring me back to their website time and time again. I expressed a genuine dissatisfaction with the wait times, how I was being nickeled-and-dimed (a twelve-dollar fee just to pick your seat), and other concerns. The agent huffed to the point where I could see her rolling her eyes through the telephone. I then had specific questions about the hotel I booked through the airline's website, and I was transferred to a separate vacations department and placed on hold again. Receiving equally bad service from that department, I proceeded to cancel my entire reservation and rebook with the more well-known carrier.

That was my first and *last* experience doing business with this airline. Everything spoke to the experience: the unacceptable hold time, unfriendly agents, the nickeling-and-diming, and the transferring from department to department. All of this spoke negatively to me, the customer. What message is being sent with this kind of service? Further, what kind of message is being sent to the employees who have to deliver it? For the customer, it says, "We don't need or want you." To the employee, it says they are not smart or trusted enough to be entrusted with the ability to take care of customer concerns. I can't even begin to imagine what kind of work culture prevails at the call center for this airline. If the employees are that unbecoming to customers, imagine how they are to one another.

I don't play video games much. I grew up with a classic Nintendo system and spent many hours playing *Castlevania* and *Tetris*. I miss the days of two buttons on the control pad versus the multiple buttons on gaming systems today. Modern games are often difficult with multiple levels and objectives to achieve. With that said, there are a few I really do enjoy. One of my absolute favorites is a game released in 2014 called *Alien Isolation*. It is a survivalist mode game based off the *Alien* movie franchise that Sigourney Weaver made famous. Just in case you have never heard of this series, the original movie debuted with all all-star cast in 1979 about a dangerous xenomorph alien that invaded a spaceship and horribly killed the crew within hours of its arrival. I believe it to be one of the scariest movies of any genre. I still jump in my seat when watching Sigourney Weaver's character running through dark hallways while being chased by this hideous creature.

Without going into in-depth story lines, the premise of this game is to evade one of these alien creatures on board a space station. The player is not able to kill the creature, but rather can only avoid it. And what makes it even more difficult is the game utilizes artificial intelligence technology which enables the alien creature to learn your playing habits and adjust accordingly.

Every conceivable detail was imagined, transporting the player into the world of *Alien*. The design of the space station resembles that of the original movie. It accurately portrays what director Ridley Scott envisioned as the future in the late 1970's. The sounds, the lighting, the architecture of the game are spot on to the original movie and are a great tribute to the series.

So, what does playing video games have to do with customer experience? Even though I have played the game to completion multiple times, *I keep coming back to enjoy it*. I still get scared playing it. I jump at moments that I know are coming. I appreciate all the hundreds, if not thousands, of hidden design features to make it more real for me. Everything speaks to the effort these game designers put into making this as realistic as possible. And it keeps me coming back, time and time again.

Everything makes up an experience for a customer, even the hidden details. While a video game is much different than a brick-and-mortar operation, the principles are the same. The experience you give your guests will determine if they will walk out the door and never return or become brand loyalists and give you repeat business.

A friend of mine once walked into a local business. There was a photocopied sign that read, "I can only please one person a day, and today is not your day. Tomorrow isn't looking good for you either!" Knowing my friend, I am sure he saw this sign for what it was intended to be: something funny meant to inject a little humor. That same friend recalled that another customer walked in shortly after, read the sign, and immediately left the store and went somewhere else. There is power in the messages we send. Remember, everything speaks.

The Little Things

It's amazing how the smallest entities can cause a profound impact. Microscopic germs enter our bodies, bringing everything from the flu virus to deadly pathogenic illnesses. It was the common cold virus that brought down the mighty Martians in my favorite book, *The War of the Worlds*. The smallest things can reap the biggest results.

After learning this principle, I took it to heart and implemented some little things that I thought would set the stage better for both my guests and employees. Earlier, I shared some examples of creating an inviting back-office experience for employees and reinforcing positivity and recognition when they go above and beyond. This is a crucial part of setting the stage for productive employee development.

But I didn't get into the little things that improve the customer experience. Well, here are some of those little things I implemented.

Living in a desert (which Utah is) means that in the summer it can be very hot. In this environment, people can be a little more cranky than usual. I would try to offset the uncomfortable temperatures with fresh, daily made, flavored lemonades waiting in the front lobby as people entered. I would dedicate one employee to hand out the refreshing drinks to each client that came in. I even had a special name tag made that said Vice-President of Hydration Distribution to make the employee handing them out feel a little extra special. We rotated the employees every hour, only pulling them off the drink station if things got a little busy. The nice taste of a delicious cold lemonade, followed by a sincere smile and welcome, always seemed to put a smile on the faces of even the most upset customers.

I will talk later about the legendary customer service of Nordstrom, but I heard a story about them when I attended Zappos culture-development program. A customer walked into a Nordstrom to purchase a dress shirt. Apparently, the man was attending a wedding and had spilled a beverage on his only dress shirt. He was in a rush to make it back to continue his duties as best man. The shirt was pinned up and folded in a fancy box, looking like a complex origami piece. The Nordstrom employee rang up the shirt and told the customer, "I will be right back." A few minutes later, out came the employee with a freshly ironed and pressed dress shirt for the customer so he would look his best. This was a classic touch of service, a little thing that made the experience extra special.

Another example that proved to be surprisingly successful was my time as a manager of a grocery branch of a major national bank. Anyone who is reading this who has worked at an in-store banking location knows the struggles these banking professionals face. In-store banks are probably the *least* successful locations of a financial institution. This is for a variety of reasons but mainly because customers have a perception that in-store offices don't offer all the full services of their brick-and-mortar counterparts, and most customers shopping at a grocery store want to be left alone. My team and I had to come up with a new way to stand out among other competing banks in the area, one being in the same parking lot as our location. Our bank engaged in a promotion every quarter where new customers would receive seventy-five dollars to open a checking account. Being a grocery store, this presented a fantastic and untapped opportunity to reach out to people. I decided to shift the first point of customer contact away from the actual branch location tucked between the magazines and the pharmacy and make the first point of contact the bank employees and the promotion itself. So, we rotated every hour, going into the store and walking up to random people and inviting them to let *us* be their personal shoppers and put seventy-five dollars' worth of groceries in their cart. Then, right before checkout, we would escort them over to the branch location, sign up their account, issue a debit card, and then pay for their groceries. Then, as a final icing on the cake, we would assist the often-forgotten bagger in putting everything into bags and would conclude by taking out the groceries to the new happy customer's vehicle. Did some people take advantage of this promotion? You bet! Did some people close the account as soon as their groceries were bought and paid for? Sure did! But we must remember the cost of doing business. Most people were appreciative of our commitment to service and returned to our bank for their future financial needs. Once, a young mother of three broke down in tears when we offered to pay for her groceries around Thanksgiving, as she had recently lost her job and was struggling to make ends meet. To us, offering to pay for groceries was a little thing, but for that customer, it was a life-changing experience.

I once stayed at a very impressive resort in Arizona. The sight was something that caused my jaw to drop, driving up the long entrance to the porte cochere. From the gorgeous landscaping to the backdrop of the desert mountains, it was a sight to be seen. Upon check-in, my bags were taken by a bellman and advanced to my room to be ready and waiting when I arrived. I was then personally escorted around the major focal points of the hotel by a concierge ambassador to become familiar with all the amenities and better maximize the enjoyment of my stay. Finally, after a detailed tour, I was brought back to the main lobby, where a Native American chief blessed my stay at the property with a traditional prayer and song. Talk about a welcome! All these little things that I experienced made my stay truly memorable. And I certainly was nothing special. I was not a VIP, or a corporate executive, or a politician. This level of service is delivered to every guest of the hotel, regardless of your room size, bank account, or standing in society. To them, you are their *guest*, the most important person to them for the moments you are together.

One of the best experiences with a little thing was at Chick-fil-A. This company sets impressive customer-service standards. But what makes this company unique is its use of the little things tool in the customer-service toolbox. I was going through a particularly difficult time personally. After being fired from the financial institution, I was doing temporary work to make ends meet. There were some very heavy thoughts on my mind, and emotionally, I was drained. I drove up to my local Chick-fil-A restaurant and placed my usual order: a sausage and egg biscuit, hash browns, and a small soft drink. I order that meal every time I go to Chick-fil-A for breakfast. The young ladies who work the drive-through window every morning always seem to remember me, often greeting me with "Welcome back" as I drive up to the window. This morning though, they took it a step further. I am sure my facial expression reflected my mood that morning: defeated and on the verge of tears. I pulled up, proceeded to give the familiar employee my credit card, and then received an undeserved and unexpected gift. The young lady took my debit card. However, she came right back with it and my bag containing my hot and fresh meal. She then said with a smile, "You know what? It's on the house today." I was stunned. With a blank stare, I remember asking why I was being singled out for this rare treat. With a smile, she responded, "You come here almost every morning. We just want you to know that we appreciate you and hope you have a great rest of the day!" With that, I could not hold back my emotions, as I let loose the waterworks in my car. Those darn onions again! It was truly a moment I will never forget as a customer. As a Christian company, I am sure Chick-fil-A would assert that the employee was using the promptings of the Holy Spirit in that decision to gift me with a free meal. Maybe it was just her good heart. Maybe she saw I was not in the best state of mind and just used her good customer-service training and instincts. Maybe it was a combination of things. Whatever the case, I am sure it was a very little thing to that nice employee. For me, it was a life-changing interaction.

I love these simple, beautiful stories where someone took the initiative to go above and beyond to provide amazing service. None of these actions were necessary or required. Rather, they are the results of service-driven individuals and organizations that live and breathe the values they promote.

The Story within the Scene

We should think of service as various scenes in a movie that speak differently depending on the audience. I know for myself when I watch a movie, I will often take away a message or theme much differently than a friend of mine or the stranger sitting several rows down from me. Employee empowerment is crucial so on-the-fly decisions can be made in order to adapt the scene to the individual guest. For example, the same luxury resort in Arizona I spoke of earlier actively encourages its guests to have a glass of wine and sample fresh cheese around the fire each night. But what if you're a nondrinker? This would come off as very intrusive. So, the hotel offers alternatives of sparkling cider and nonalcoholic drinks upon request, equally emphasizing a spirit of community.

A great example of employee empowerment and scene setting is told by Micah Solomon about an experience at one of Garret Harker's famous Boston area restaurants:

> We had an upcoming wedding shower scheduled at Eastern Standard Kitchen & Drinks. Unfortunately, one of the brides invited guests was suffering from a severe form of cancer that kept her from eating solid foods. My staff met on their own accord and created an all liquid menu for her to enjoy in tandem with other guests … they came up with an amazing chilled corn chowder that tasted as though they'd extracted the essence of corn, fresh from the field, and poured it into a glass.[11]

Scene setting goes for smaller, individual customer touch points. A customer who has been driving all night and arrives at a hotel at 1:30 a.m. will need a very different scene set for them compared to the wide-awake family of four who arrives at 3:00 p.m. A customer who is hard of hearing will need a very different scene set for them than a hard-of-sight customer. A newly engaged couple on a cruise ship wants a very different scene set for them than a traveling family with little children. Disney took this into account on their cruise ships. There are sections of the ships that are designated for adults only, children only, and family only. This is expanded to their private Caribbean island known as Castaway Cay. Now each segment of the customer demographic can have a specific and individual experience. Adults can relax in the peace and quiet of their own areas, families can enjoy some time together, and children can have fun in a supervised environment.

The Waiting Game

Anyone who has been to a busy bank branch knows that sometimes the wait in line can be extensive. To take a note from the Disney Institute playbook, Walt Disney knew that people would have to wait in lines before experiencing the actual thrill of the attraction. So, he imagined the waiting line as being part of the attraction. What a fantastic concept! He wanted the queue to be as memorable as the ride itself. That is why when one goes to a Disney park, they are overwhelmed by the details of the queue to fit with the theme of the ride. I know as a kid, I got a real kick out of seeing my pre-departure travel videos on Star Tours or watching the clips of *The Twilight Zone* on the Tower of Terror ride. Recently, Disney took it a step further by creating interactive contact points within the wait queue. This is explained by Theodore Kinni:

> Guests riding the Haunted Mansion will now find an expansion to the graveyard they pass on their way into the main house. Elaborate crypts with interactive features have been added. When guests reach the tomb of a music composer, they find instruments carved into it. Touch it, and the music begins to play.[12]

Why make such an investment in a line queue? "Guests were *willing to wait* twelve percent longer because of the interactive experience," explained Walt Disney resorts and parks Vice President Lori Georganna.[13] Priorities need to be set for the delivery system experience. Your customers will see those priorities in how they are treated. Is a customer's positive experience more important than stocking shelves? Is decreasing wait time more important than fixing a display case? Only you can decide that. But there are little things that can be done to prioritize the customer experience during long wait times. Perhaps an employee can hand out snacks with a sincere "Thank you for your patience!" to customers as they stand in line. That can be followed up with an additional "Thank you for your patience" once a customer arrives at the bank teller window, or checkout register, or whatever the case might be for your business. This expresses to a customer that you recognize their time is valuable and have acknowledged the inconvenience. Or perhaps you can cross-train all your employees to run your POS system. When the line starts to back up, pull them from their stock room or inventory duties so they can better assist getting customers through the line. Or, you can think outside the box, as a fellow bank manager did. His branch was notoriously busy, especially the drive-up teller lanes.

During long wait times, this manager would personally go out into the lanes with a bottle of glass cleaner and several rolls of paper towels and would proceed to wash the windows of waiting cars. It was his small way of turning a long wait time (and thus a negative experience) into a memorable and positive one.

Setting the Stage Behind the Scenes

I love watching reruns of the shows *Kitchen Nightmares* and *Hotel Hell*, featuring the infamous chef Gordon Ramsey. One of the first questions the chef would ask the owner of the establishment is, "When was the last time you ate/stayed here?" And almost every time, the person would respond with a "seldom" or "never" response. That would open an endless tirade of swear words, slurs, and insults from the chef on setting standards and of seeing things from the guest's perspective. Take away the obviously scripted swearing and pre-agreed-upon boorishness, and Ramsey is exactly right. Everyone, from the person who cleans the floor to the president, needs to experience the organization they work for not as an employee but as a consumer. They must step out of their role as the senior executive and transform themselves into the customer purchasing the product or service and see if it matches the experience they tout and promote behind the scenes.

A manager or senior executive should experience their organization not only from the perspective of the customer but also from that of the direct report employee. One thing that would make me so frustrated in the banking industry (and many frontline workers/managers in other industries can relate) was when the higher-ups made the rounds, as if the king was checking in on his subjects to ensure they were carrying out his various edicts. The district or regional manager made their token yearly checkups to hear the concerns of both customers and employees, to then report those concerns to senior management (that's the theory, anyway). In reality, they are making meaningless and required duty calls in the name of good management, not valuing the concerns of those who know firsthand what it's like to keep the company in business. Maybe that is why I fell in love with the show *Undercover Boss*. Take away the predictable endings where the boss would reward the "unsuspecting" employee with a promotion or much-needed vacation, and what remained was an insightful and sincere attempt to understand an organization from the top down. In fact, I wish more corporate CEOs, COOs, and other senior-management executives would take the time to spend time on the front lines of their businesses, to truly understand the needs of both the guest and the employee. I was impressed by how these senior executives genuinely implemented changes to the organization after seeing and experiencing problems firsthand. For example, a CEO of a large Jamaican fast-food organization on the East Coast was informed of a defective and out-of-date product-ordering system. The local restaurant would put in requests to the home office, only to find that it took weeks to receive an answer. The CEO saw that this was unacceptable and not only changed the process but hired the person who pointed out the problem as a consultant! Another example was a CEO of a national hotel chain who shadowed a front desk manager. The manager stated that guests expressed genuine concerns and suggestions to improve their guest experience, but those concerns never made it to the home office. So, the CEO created a direct Office of the President department, staffed by a few talented, service-oriented individuals who would take down the concerns of guests and report those directly to the CEO once a week.

In both examples, the outcome resulted in a healing of the gaping rift between an organization and its senior leaders in a home office usually thousands of miles away. But this not only applies to large corporations with tens of thousands of employees. It is as true for the small business in a strip mall as it is for the billion-dollar entity. Workers employed by large corporations expect some kind of disconnect due to the large nature of the organization. They expect answers to take little longer, requests to be granted with a little more delay, and for there to be some level of bureaucratic red tape. I am not saying that it is right, but that is generally the case. What is most frustrating, however, is when the employees of smaller organizations have direct access to the owner or senior manager, and little to nothing is discussed or resolved. Nothing ever happens from the bottom up but only from the top down. When the owner wears the king-of-the-castle crown, high turnover and employee disconnect inevitably follow shortly after.

As a manager myself, I take this challenge everywhere I go. I use every interaction as a learning experience. I make internal notes of what was positive about the interaction and what could use some improvement. I look back and say to myself, "I would never do that if I was in that position" or "That is definitely something I need to implement!" I compare every organization I interact with, identifying the various points of contact and making a rough analysis at the end.

Earlier, we discussed creating a positive work culture. Productivity and production increase when your employees feel valued. It is a scientific fact. As mentioned previously, when employees feel valued and that their opinions matter, they feel genuinely invested in the workplace and strive to do better to improve sales, processes, and operations. In chapter 4, I shared the experience of watching a video about Royal Caribbean cruise lines and their commitment to setting a backstage as equal to the front. In that same chapter, I shared the importance of treating employees as more than just employees. Setting the stage is not just about appearances and service; it is also a process in which a service is executed. One cannot stand without the other, as both are equally important and require equal commitment.

The Back-Office Problem

I will speak about this in depth later, but large organizations with a vast enterprise of operations often run into the back-office problem. This is caused when departments fails to convey a customer first mentality across all the enterprise regardless if they are customer facing. Many organizations believe that because a certain role is not primarily customer facing, the level of service should be adjusted. This could not be further from the truth.

I mentioned earlier being a manager for twenty-four various locations of a large western United States regional bank. This financial institution loved to promote how it has never forgotten the customers who keep them in business. But sadly, most of the time, this was nothing more than a tagline on a billboard. It was rarely enforced as a practice. Having to interact with the back office was about as much fun as going to the dentist. I dreaded picking up the phone and calling one of many behind-the-scenes departments.

One thing that frustrated me as a bank manager was when some fellow managers put employees into what I call a job box; the loan officer only works on loans, the drive-up teller only helps drive-up customers, and so forth. I promoted a concept that a team works together to have one another's backs and to make the process as efficient as possible for the customer. I know from experience how frustrating it is to walk into a busy bank branch and see a large line for the tellers and then see several employees standing around, not offering to assist. So, I made sure that during peak times, every employee was available to assist with teller transactions if they were not already engaged with another customer. My loan officers had check deposit scanners at their desks, so I mandated that loan officers and personal bankers assist with noncash deposits during busy times. I directed the drive-through tellers to assist the lobby tellers with transactions while not assisting our valued drive-up customers. This created not only a positive customer experience but a spirit of cooperation and teamwork among the employees. I would not allow the "it's not my assigned job" mentality, for I believe that attitude is a leading cause of workplace dysfunction and cultural inefficiency.

While a manager at this same bank, I had a client who was taking out a home equity line of credit. Believe it or not, it was to take his family to Disneyland (so you see, people really do that!). His two sons were preparing to go away for two years on religious missionary assignments, and he wanted to have a memorable family vacation. The client needed the money accessible by a certain day, so we pulled strings to get appraisals ordered quicker and titles conveyed faster than usual. We were one day away from closing when the back office sent me the final documents they were in charge of preparing. Upon review, I found that the interest rate disclosed was different from the one quoted. It was a small clerical error. However, no one wanted to take responsibility for the problem. I was informed that the documents had to go back to the initial underwriter for review, who then had to give permission for it to be changed, which in turn started the process over again from the beginning. I was transferred to several departments on the phone, each one with a "not my responsibility" mind-set. I was told that the changes could take an additional three days. This was unacceptable! Finally, I had to appeal to a senior vice president to get a minor clerical error fixed. Something that should have taken five minutes to fix ended up taking almost four hours.

Talk about a nightmare. This could have been so much easier for everyone involved had the cultural mentality been in favor of the customer. In this case, the back office was more concerned with shifting blame than keeping the commitment to the customer. What should have happened in this case was for a back-office representative to take responsibility for the error and shift into resolution mode.

The best example of this is when I was a senior director of auto finance. I often had to communicate with this automaker's financing bank, and each time, it was like pulling teeth. For the purpose of this story, I will refer to the automotive bank as ABC Financial and will not use the real names of the people I spoke with. I will also use a fake name for the business. I had a situation where I needed to obtain a vehicle payoff for a vehicle leased in the name of a business. My customer was purchasing his business truck at the end of the lease period. I called the only number on file, and the conversation went something like this:

"Thank you for calling ABC Financial. This call is being recorded for quality control. My name is Sally."

"Yes, my name is Bryan, and I need to obtain a lease payoff for Bob's Towing Company."

"Okay, so if I am understanding this right, you need a business lease payoff?"

"Yes."

"Just a moment." Then came the annoying hold music and wait time. "I unfortunately am not able to assist you. This is consumer leasing. Let me transfer you." More hold music followed with a five-minute hold time.

"Thank you for calling ABC Financial. This call is being recorded for quality control. My name is Sarah."

"Yes, my name is Bryan, and I need to obtain a lease payoff for Bob's Towing Company."

"Unfortunately, this is the business retail department. I will need to transfer you to the business lease department." At this point, my blood pressure began to rise. But I patiently waited again through the hold music and another lengthy queue.

"Thank you for calling ABC Financial. This call is being recorded for quality control. My name is Adam."

"Yes, my name is Bryan, and I need to obtain a lease payoff for Bob's Towing Company."

"Unfortunately, I am not able to assist you with that information. This is the business title department. You will need to speak to someone in business leasing." My face began to turn red at this point. I explained to the agent my frustration in being informed from the previous agent that I was being transferred to business leasing. "No, I am sorry. I am not able to assist you. Let me transfer you." More hold music and another long wait queue.

"Thank you for calling ABC Financial. This call is being recorded for quality control. My name is Paul."

"Yes, my name is Bryan, and for the love of God I need a simple business lease payoff for Bob's Freaking Towing Company!"

Seventeen minutes and forty-five seconds later, I got my payoff, which took the agent thirty seconds to generate on his computer. I was frustrated at the complete lack of customer commitment from this bank. This was a horrible experience not only for me but for the guest as well. My customer had to sit in our lobby for seventeen extra unnecessary minutes for a simple lease payoff. Because the customer was not in front of these phone agents, there was no sense of urgency. There was no commitment to customer experience. Any thought of being a team player and assisting me was out of the question. I was just one of thousands of employees serving one of thousands of customers. That was the mind-set of this large organization, and it is the mind-set of many large corporate operations.

These examples demonstrate why it is so crucial for organizations to implement policies and practices that encourage a spirit of true teamwork, that working together to take care of the customer should be the sole purpose of the organization.

Customer Service vs. Customer Experience

Scholars and professionals have attempted to define the difference between the service a customer receives compared to the actual experience they have. While there are countless opinions, not one is definitive. In my opinion, simply put, customer experience is the *complete* interaction a customer has with a brand or organization. It is what determines if your customers flock to competitors or stay loyal to your brand. Customer service, on the other hand, is the actual completion of a transaction and the people involved in making it possible. A prime example would be a customer walking into a grocery store, picking out a gallon of milk, paying for the item to a clerk, and leaving the store. It was a transactional situation. It added up like a simple math problem: A + B + C = D. I needed milk, and thus I got it. Someone had to ring up the item, I had to hand over cash, it was put in a bag and I left.

But it can't just end there. In fact, the research tells us just the opposite. The experience of a customer is the most crucial aspect of the transaction. It is about doing what the customer expected and looking for chances to exceed those expectations.

In the example above, did the clerk warmly welcome me to the checkout line? Did they smile? Did they ask me how my day was going? Did they inquire if I needed anything additional? Did they thank me for my business and invite me to come back? Did they offer to take my groceries to my car? Was the storefront clean and orderly? These are the little things that make up the experience, not just the transaction itself.

In this modern experience driven economy, it is the responsibility of every team member at an organization to work together for the benefit of the customer. Consumers have more choices than ever before. There are multiple sources to obtain the same product or service. And with the advent of social media, consumers are more aware than ever before. They will make determinations about your organization without ever stepping through the doors of it. They are using reviews and customer recommendations to decide if they want to do business with you. This has created a battlefield you must conquer in order to win and keep customers; the weapon of choice is customer experience. The experience your customers have will be the determining factor.

Forbes magazine reports, "80% of companies believe they deliver super experiences, but only 8% of customers actually agree. In other words, companies have a long way to go."[14]

The race to own the customer experience is in full swing. Research firm PWC found that 86% of customers are willing to pay more for a product or service if they have a great experience to match.[15] Companies must recognize the importance of delivering an experience that makes them stand out from their competition. But the door swings both ways on this one. While companies will be remembered for the exceptional service they provide, the same is also true for the less than pleasant and even downright horrific experiences they render. Remember how the video of a doctor who was beaten and hauled off a United Airlines flight went viral in less than twenty-four hours? Remember when Wells Fargo was caught defrauding its customers and causing financial havoc for millions? Remember when Bill Heard Auto Group was shut down by the government for unlawful and deceptive sales practices? Horrible experiences like these speak loudly, and will be at the forefront of customers' minds as they decide whether to keep doing business with a brand. Your brand needs to stand out in people's minds for all the right reasons.

Digital Customer Touch Points

These details don't just extend to the in-person experience, but to all delivery systems within your organization. Websites, mobile applications, and even call centers should be committed to providing an unmatched customer experience.

I remember visiting the Disney website to inquire about a vacation package. There was a feature built into its coding where the site could detect the specific time zone I was in, and it adjusted its colors and theme to match the current time of day. So, I was logging into the site around 8:30 p.m., and the site knew that. The site darkened, with stars shining on the banner page, as if to invoke a nighttime setting. As I browsed the page, a small shooting star would shoot across the computer screen. A minor, minor detail but a powerful one at that!

Amazon has taken this concept to a whole new level. One of the little things enacted by this e-commerce giant is photo delivery. I admit I am not one who uses Amazon as religiously as others. On the few occasions I have used an e-commerce site, my number one concern is delivery when I am absent. Amazon shared this concern and adjusted accordingly. Now, shoppers can have a photo taken of their item being delivered and the location it was delivered, which in turn helps customers see when and where the package was delivered.

Amazon has also addressed the growing nationwide problem of "porch pirates" taking other customers items that have been dropped off when they are not home. Amazon is working to place lockers in most major metropolitan cities. Customers can direct delivery drivers to drop off packages in these secure lockers versus leaving them out in the open at a place of residence. And the service is free for Prime members.

Companies are expected to deliver an online/multichannel experience on par with their face-to-face interactions. Doing business online is the new normal. Live chat, email, call centers and websites are just some of the multiple channels a customer can utilize. When it comes to providing a positive experience across different channels, the mobile app/website experience is now expected to be the primary and possibly only time a customer will interact with your company. Therefore, it needs to be the best experience possible. According to research, 57% of customers surveyed won't recommend a business with a poorly designed website or mobile application. And if a website isn't mobile-friendly, half of your customers will stop visiting it, even if they like the business.[16]

I mention again my very good HR friend. He shared with me a little thing that he encountered using a website, which in turn was a negative experience. He was contacting a vendor who supplies awards for city employees. As Christmas was approaching soon, it was crucial that certain awards were lined up and ready for the end-of-the-year banquet. The product representative of this company was out of town, and my friend was directed to the online chat service. He explained to the agent that he needed help. He was the key holder of the vendor's awards website and needed some additional online access granted for certain city employees. The online agent simply referred him back to his representative. That was not going to work, as the representative would be out of town for quite some time. My friend was directed to the email of an individual and politely asked the agent to forward the chat to the correct individual. Without a response, next thing he knew he was reading, "Your chat session has been disconnected".

My friend shared his frustration with me. "What good is a company if they can't/won't help me?" His experience sadly continued to worsen. He emailed the referred individual but was directed to start over again and explain the problem from the beginning. My friend summed it up best: "My request is not difficult. I need someone to give me access!"

This is a little thing that speaks adversely to the customer experience. There is not a person in America who has not contacted an organization, waited in a queue, explained the situation, been placed again on hold, been informed they have the wrong department, are then been transferred to another department and finally met with "So I can better understand, will you explain the nature of your problem?" *Gast! I just spent the last twenty minutes explaining it to the last person!*

What good is having multiple delivery systems if you're just going to give your customers the run around? If you're going to deliver a multi-channel experience, then it must be on par with the overall customer experience vision of your company. Don't have chat agents just for the sake of having chat agents. Rather, give them the same ability to remedy customer's concerns as you would a front-line employee. How effective is it to have the expense of implementing a live chat application and agent if they can't do anything to solve the problem? While customers will allow themselves to be serviced from different channels, they also expect the experience remain consistent. They want a memorable experience regardless if they are talking to a human in person, on the phone, or over a chat application.

In their 2020 survey, PWC Research found the number of companies investing in the omni-channel experience has jumped from 20% to more than 80%.[17] There is a tremendous benefit to multi-channel contact, especially live chat interactions. Live chat software helps to communicate instantly and avoids long wait times. *If* done right, 92% of customers will have a positive view of a company when the online chat experience resulted in the customer having their issue resolved quickly and professionally.[18] The conversations can be made interactive by using face-to-face video and co-browsing for a better live chat customer experience. Perhaps this is why many banks and credit unions have integrated video banking into their mobile applications and ATM machines.

But these interactions must be personal. Standard responses like "We understand your frustration" are viewed as impersonal and uncaring. If real people are going to work your chat and mobile apps, they need to infuse a little of their personality into the conversation. Offer real empathy and understanding to the concern, use affirming language such as "Let me take care of that for you", and end by offering to follow up with the customer to make sure all their needs were met. You can refer to that Zappos email an agent sent as a reference on how to provide personalized interactions over e-mail or chat channels.

In the story my friend shared, an employee who worked in a service-driven culture would have been empowered to remedy the problem right then and there. They would have apologized for the error and used affirming language such as, "Absolutely! Once I verify your security credentials, I will be happy to grant you immediate access." They would have taken ownership of the situation and followed up to make sure everything was working correctly. At the very least, they would have forwarded the conversation to the appropriate individual and advised them of the situation.

Empowering employees to say yes to customers is imperative during all customer-facing interactions. A service-focused culture enables employees to get the job done. A bottom-line-focused organization hides in layers of red tape and excuses. Little things speak volumes to how you value your customers. Did my friend's interaction lay out the welcome mat for him? Did it scream, "Prego!"? Did it remind him that his city's business was appreciated and needed? What message are you sending through the little things and quiet whispers within your organization? Disney might be able to afford a shooting star on its website. Maybe you can't. But granting employees the access to take care of customers is a very little thing that costs you little, and yields amazing results.

Bottom Line: You may be saying to yourself, "All of this attention to detail is a lot of hard work!" Well, you would be exactly right. Creating a memorable experience is hard work. Business is hard work. Life is hard work. Disney's John Hench said it best:

> "Its attention to infinite detail, the little things, the little, minor, picky points that others just don't want

to take the time, money, or effort to do. As far as our Disney organization is concerned, it's the only way we've ever done it!"[19]

This concept is not something that can be done part of the time. You either are fully invested in creating this type of experience, or you're not. As Yoda famously says, "Do, or do not; there is no try." The little things like offering your guests a bottle of water upon entry or the quiet whisper of a shooting star on a website can make or break the customer experience. Equally important is the stage you set for your employees. Do they have open, direct access to senior leaders and management for honest communication? Are their concerns and suggestions genuinely taken into consideration? Do they feel valued, needed, and appreciated? Do you train your back-of-house operations to have the same mind-set as front-facing employees? Do they truly remember that the sole purpose of the organization is to create a positive experience for the customer? Take a moment to really evaluate your operation and the ways it can improve the customer experience across all channels.

Chapter 6

Thank You, Come Again!

"The key is to set realistic customer expectations, and then not to just meet them, but to *exceed* them." – Sir Richard Branson

I WANT YOU TO close your eyes and think for a moment of a company in an industry that drives you completely mad when dealing with them. Maybe it's an airline, insurance company, utility company, or cell phone provider. I know, for me, a tie at the top of the list is airlines and cell phone providers. The others rank close, but these two take the cake when it comes to providing notoriously bad service.

Give Customers a Reason to Come Back

I had to call a megacorporation to have an issue resolved. After waiting on hold for twenty-five minutes, I finally reached a person who I could clearly tell wanted to get me off the phone as soon as possible. Literally, the answer to every question or request was "No!" or the dreaded "Unfortunately..." I finally said, tongue in cheek but semiseriously, "Is there anything you *can* do for me, besides take my money and provide bad service?" The call didn't progress much further after that, and I discontinued my business with that company.

Whatever you choose to call them (guests/customers/clients), people today want a genuine experience more than ever. They crave sincere human interaction and memorable experiences. They want a reason to come back to your place of business. The question is simple: will you give them one? Theodore Kinney of the Disney Institute states the following:

> Underneath the trappings of every organization, we are all driving toward the same goal: serving the people who purchase and use our products and services. We all must satisfy our guests—and convince them to return and recommend us to others—or risk losing them in the long run.[1]

It is unfortunate how organizations have adopted a "too big to fail" mindset. They do not see the customer as an essential part of their business. Rather, they see a customer as a disposable commodity. In a simpler time, the customer was the engine that drove business. Everything revolved around him/her. Sam Walton modeled his future retail empire off this belief. He understood the customer held the power to control the destiny of a company, from the president to the cashier. This power was exercised by the customer simply taking their business elsewhere. In his time, every customer was respected and appreciated. Today, it is just the opposite.

I think it would be accurate to say that most consumers rarely feel valued when they interact with an organization. I seldom feel like a business genuinely wants me to come back and use their product or service again. Today, actions speak louder than words. Any organization can thank us and ask us to come back and go through the standard motions of customer service. But did their *actions* confirm that sentiment? If an organization puts a mission statement on the wall touting how much it cares about customers, then the entire experience should reflect that. Simply asking the customer to return is no longer enough; it must be *proven* through the entire interaction.

The Power of Yes

Now, I am sure I am not explaining anything new here. A lot of industry professionals have heard of the yes-driven service culture and the power behind it. Rather than reinvent the wheel, I am going to share a few examples. But just in case there are some of you who have never heard of this concept, I will briefly recap.

Saying yes is a service standard principle where the customer has their expectations exceeded simply by doing what they asked. It seems like a radical concept now. As consumers, we generally expect the answer and the experience to say no. Companies are going to nickel-and-dime us and hide behind policies that favor them. It's what we have come to expect and count on. That is why when a company goes above and beyond to say yes and make it happen, it is a forever memorable experience for the client.

Richard Branson understands this idea. I love one of his stories about what inspired him to implement this at his hotels. He explains that when he would go to conventional hotels, he would notice the phone had six to seven different buttons for various departments, such as the housekeeper or the bellman. He recalls picking up the phone and waiting for someone to pick up. He would be transferred around until someone could resolve the issue. Branson decided to put one button on his hotel phones. You guessed it: "YES!" is at the top of every phone in bold red letters. Branson has set a service philosophy and culture throughout his organization that everyone is empowered to serve the guest. No matter who answers the phone, they are enabled to get it done for the guest.

Sometimes we have to say no because the demand or request of the customer is simply over the top. In the banking world, this is usually found in the form of customers asking for fees returned due to over drafting. But I made it a practice with myself and my employees to always look for opportunities to turn a no into a yes. One great example is a personal banker employee I had the pleasure of working with. A customer of the bank came into our location to change the pin on his debit card. Regrettably, our machine was broken and was being serviced. We had to direct the customer ten minutes down the road to another location. This was a definite no experience for the customer, so my banker took it up a notch and turned it into a yes. My banker examined the customer's driver's license and saw the word *veteran* in big letters. After thanking him for his service to our country and asking which branch of the military he was in, my banker proceeded to check the customer's account type. The banker noticed the customer had our most basic account type. My banker turned on his service standards and upgraded the customer to a military account, which comes with the best features and benefits. The customer walked away happier than when he entered.

Another example involves another personal banker at a different location I managed. I was working at the teller line, and a client approached him. It was an older female who was alone and looked mildly confused. She asked my employee to assist her with some problems setting up a PayPal account. Now, I don't know the first thing about PayPal. We as a bank did not have access to their systems. We had to say no, that we were not PayPal and could not assist her directly. But my banker felt bad for this woman who obviously needed some help. So, we turned on our service mentality and together contacted PayPal and were able to assist in providing her routing and account number. We printed off instructions for her in case she needed help in the future. Was it something we had to do? Absolutely not. Was it the right thing to do? Yes! In both cases, the employee could have easily just said no and moved on to the next person. And they would not necessarily have been wrong for doing so. But by having a service mentality, they could not just leave it at that. They looked for an opportunity to turn a negative situation into an amazing experience.

Another story I learned at the Ritz-Carlton Institute was about a phone agent at a large telecommunications company who was on hold with a customer for quite some time. There was a substantial problem that required many hours of phone and remote support. The customer was understandably frustrated, tired, and *hungry*. The customer, however, could not hang up the phone since the agent was remoted into the home computer to resolve the issue. The agent felt compelled to act. While on the phone, the agent placed an order online for a pizza to be delivered. Before either of them knew it, the doorbell was ringing, and the customer broke down crying because of the kindness shown by a stranger over the phone.

Some people think that you need to have an amazing interaction or experience to qualify as life-changing or to be worthy of corporate recognition. Saying yes ultimately means resolving customer concerns. It means going just a little bit above and beyond to help, to be of service, or to bring a smile to someone's face. Saying yes is anticipating a need before it is even mentioned. It is using sound, empowered judgment to take the customer touch point from ordinary to extraordinary. It is simply doing what the customer asks to be done; it's not rocket science!

I Have Always Wanted a Pony

The story that transformed my beliefs about service was told by Micah Solomon. He tells of when he was at the Four Seasons Resort in Austin, Texas. The friendly concierge clerk asked, "Is there anything else I can do to make your stay more enjoyable?" Micah wanted to put the service standards of this report to the test. So he responded, "You know, I've always wanted a pony!" Without hesitation, the agent sprang into action. "I'll get right to work on that for you!" Within an hour, the agent had provided a list of ponies available for purchase in the local area, along with veterinarians, trainers, and tack and feed stores. The clerk even offered to take him to the location of his choice via the hotel limo. She enabled the guest to accomplish his goal by going above and beyond what was expected.[2]

A great story demonstrating this occurred when I was supervising a teller at a local branch. For the purpose of this story, I will call her Melissa. She was a well-sought-out employee. Clients would wait in line just for her. She was kind, remembered customers' names, and engaged in genuine conversation. One client in particular (I will call him Roy) came in regularly. Roy was older in years but incredibly young in spirit. During the winter months, he would always wear a particular scarf. It was sentimental to him, as it was a gift from his late wife. He missed her terribly, and the scarf was one of his few truly precious assets. One day, he came into our location distraught, stating his car had been broken into while in the parking lot of a grocery store that the bank shared. He asked if he could contact the local authorities. He then went on to explain how the scarf had been left in his car and was missing. Sure enough, the unkind thief took the precious heirloom along with other items.

Without hesitation, Melissa sprang into action as if was a part of her normal banking procedures. She quickly asked fellow bank employees to each contribute ten dollars so she could buy Roy a new scarf. She asked me if it was permissible to leave the bank for about a half hour, which I granted (as if she even needed to ask). She got into her car, money in hand, and drove down the road to a popular nationwide clothing retailer. She came back with a new scarf in a beautiful gift bag. She asked each employee to sign a small card. By the time she finished gathering the signatures, the police were finishing up their investigation and asking Roy to sign some paperwork. Melissa squatted down as Roy was sitting in a chair, still visibly upset and understandably emotional. She said, "I know we can never replace your wife's scarf. But we all hope this will help make your day a little brighter and a little better." With that simple act, you would think someone began to cut stale onions. Everyone was crying! I am pretty sure even the stone-faced police officer was getting emotional.

Nordstrom Sells Tires?

The best story involving customer service standards is the infamous story about a guy, four tires, and a Nordstrom parking lot. Maybe you have heard this one before. After all, if you enter "Nordstrom tires" into a search engine, you will come back with more than 1,680,000 results.

In 1975, so the story goes, a man bought four tires from a shop. A few weeks later, the brand-new tires were already defective. When the man returned to the shop, he was shocked to find it had been closed and demolished, and a Nordstrom store was up in its place. The man went into Nordstrom, explained the situation, and walked out with the exact amount of money he paid for the tires. Nordstrom does not sell tires, mind you. They easily could have said, "Sorry, that is not our problem." But they sprang into action and made a return customer for life.[3]

Some forty years later, people are still telling this story! Now there is some doubt regarding its validity. Some have even suggested it is a corporate conspiracy theory. Nordstrom officials, through various publications, have all confirmed the authenticity of the story. John Nordstrom himself said the following:

> Our commitment is 100-percent customer service. We are not committed to financial markets, we are not committed to real estate markets, we are not committed to a certain amount of profit. We are only committed to customer service. If we make a profit, that's great. But customer service is first. If I'm a salesperson on the floor and I know that the people who own this place are committed to customer service, then I am free to find new ways to give great customer service. I know I will never be criticized for taking care of a customer. I will only be criticized if I don't take care of a customer.[4]

My Pleasure

Now, I have strong feelings about these two little words. I believe it is a powerful tool in your customer-service arsenal. But slightly overuse it, and it can become as annoying as fingernails on a chalkboard. Ritz-Carlton began using this term with its guests, which led to Truett Kathy implementing the phrase throughout his Chick-fil-A stores. The story goes that Kathy visited a Ritz-Carlton and asked a front desk agent for directions. Kathy said, "Thank you," and the employee said, "My pleasure," afterward.[5] The founder of Chick-fil-A began to implement this practice because he wanted to convey the same level of professional, elegant service throughout his restaurants.

Now, as I said, this can be severely misused. Customers know when it is insincere. I know it is not your pleasure to unclog my toilet in my hotel room. I know it is not your pleasure to clean up my dirty table after eating. But it is *my pleasure* to serve you since you are the reason I get a paycheck. It is my pleasure to see you have a wonderful experience and return to my place of business.

Here is how I look at it. I always trained my employees to say, "My pleasure," should the customer thanks us for something for them. I could never say this, but I have always wanted to yell, "Don't you ever say thank you to me! I should be thanking you!" The customer is the reason for my business. Of all the places they could have chosen to do business, they chose this one! It is my sincere and genuine pleasure to go out of my way for them. There is no need to be robotic, saying "My pleasure" at every little action and whim. Rather, it is more of a mind-set to have as you conduct your business with customers.

Use Affirming Language

Whenever I hear supposed professionals saying, "Yeah," "Sure," "Okay," and "Mm-hmm," I visualize Elle Woods from *Legally Blonde*, portrayed by Reese Witherspoon. She uses ditzy wording like "For sure!" and "Oh my God, you guys!" Even now, I can see her flipping her blonde hair back with that sorority sister verbiage. And this is what I think of when this unprofessionalism is used in the business world.

As professionals, you should act the part. My employees, who I trained to be financial professionals, spoke as if they knew what they were talking about. I would strongly discourage unprofessional words and encourage usage of words such as "Absolutely," "Right away," and "Let me get right on that." It tells the customer that you respect their time and want to resolve the issue as soon as possible. Remember, they came in probably expecting a confrontation, a reason you could not assist them. They were prepared to hear something that started with that teeth-grinding word, *unfortunately*. Now, they are hearing positive, affirming language that assures them they will be taken care of and their needs will be met. An example would be as follows:

> Customer: Would you look up my checking account history for me?
> Banker: Absolutely! Let me take care of that for you right away.

This sounds so much better than those less-affirming, juvenile words. How we represent and present ourselves is a crucial part of the service-delivery process.

I Will Remember You

Sarah McLachlan made us all cry with her commercials for various animal abuse prevention charities while the song "In the Arms of An Angel" played in the background. You are lying to yourself if you've never shed a few tears watching these commercials. In 1996 she had another huge hit, "I Will Remember You". It doesn't have the same heart wrenching emotions as the other song, but a great customer experience lesson can be extracted from this: the power of using names in business.

There is a hilarious movie called *Liar, Liar* with Jim Carrey. This was one of his better movies. Carrey portrays a sleazy lawyer named Fletcher Reed who lies his way out of every situation and engaged in morally questionable actions to advance his career. His son, who was turning five years old, grew tired of his dad's broken promises. After breaking a promise to take him out for his birthday, Reed promised that he would attend his party that night. Of course, Carrey's character had a great reason to miss his son's birthday: he was sleeping with a company associate to advance his career. I am being totally sarcastic, of course. This was a despicable thing to do to his only child. But it is what binds the entire premise of the movie and story. So, we will run with it.

At that moment, his son made a wish that his dad would not be able to tell a lie for a period of twenty-four hours. And just like that, Fletcher was forced to tell the truth. Any attempt at lying resulted in a hilarious series of body spasms and nonsensical wordage. During his period of truth telling, an associate speaks with Fletcher. He was never able to remember the associate's name but would always fudge the truth and pretend that he did. Well that all changed when he was forced to admit he had no idea who this guy was. The associate greets him, to which Fletcher responded, "Hey there! You're not important enough to remember!"

Remembering people's names sends a message that we value them, that they are important to us. Using names of customers should be the goal of every employee. Now, this can be a challenge. I get that. I do not expect, nor does any realistic manager, for an employee to remember dozens or even hundreds of names daily. But there are systems in place that can help organizations with this important aspect of customer service.

In Woodstock, Ga there was a tire shop called Kauffman Tires. A customer walked into the store and was warmly greeted by a wonderful Southern accented woman who said, "Welcome Back, Mr. Steve!" The customer was absolutely blown away since he had not visited the store in over a year. The customer wanted to know how she remembered his name from over a year ago. The friendly woman confessed that she had a little magic up her sleeve. She revealed that the company invested in a computer program capable of looking up license plate numbers of previous customers. She entered his number as he drove in and there was Steve. By doing so, she was able to know his name by the time he walked through the front door.[6]

How freaking cool! This was a small and simple investment the company made to improve customer service. Some people can do this from memory. My hat goes off to these talented people. I had the privilege of managing a wonderful banking professional who could remember the name of every person she assisted. It was mind boggling how she was able to retain that much knowledge. "Hello Sam. Great to see you again! How was your son's soccer game the other day?" Personal, direct conversations like this were commonplace for this employee. It was no wonder to me why clients would wait several extra minutes in line for her to run their transactions. Kraig Martin, Commercial Director of Storage Vault states:

> Something as simple as calling a customer by their first name can go a long way in establishing a personal connection with someone, building a rapport and improving loyalty.[7]

Get Creative

Customer experience writer Jason Bordeaux shares a great story about a small business that got very creative to provide a great customer experience.

> Earlier this month was Pi Day–March 14th, or 3.14. I'm a bit of a math geek, so I personally get giddy about those little things. Why is this relevant to a great customer experience? Simple. A pizza company in Boston ran a promo that created a great customer experience–by offering discounted pizza pies for only $3.14. The promo was sent over email, but it was available in-store without having to pull out your phone or a coupon. The store I went to was packed, but every employee I interacted with greeted me and thanked me for coming in for the very first time. I felt appreciated and welcomed, regardless of how many customers were waiting. In Boston, where lunch options are plentiful, experiences like these matter–because I went back to my desk and told my coworkers and friends about the deal–some of whom

ended up checking out this deal for their dinner that same night.[8]

I had an experience like Jason's where a business went above and beyond with creativity to create a memorable experience for its guests.

I am a fan of the traditional men's barber shop. I love a steam towel wrapped around my face accompanied by a straight edge razor shave and a great haircut. There is a local business in Salt Lake City that offers these traditional men's grooming services. But, they are the first to admit they are a little unconventional. The shop encourages employees to be genuinely authentic. So, you will be greeted by a gentleman with maybe more tattoos or body piercings than your use to, or a woman with every color of the rainbow in her hair. But the service is top notch.

One Halloween, they decided to really think outside of the box and put on a *Sweeney Todd* themed night. If you have never heard of this world famous musical, I will fill you in. It is the beloved classic by Stephen Sondheim about a deranged barber who kills his clients in fits of anger and revenge, while Mrs. Lovett (his neighbor) cuts up the bodies and puts them into meat pies, which she then serves to the general public. Sounds lovely, right? Stop squirming in your chair and try to see my point here. The original show was made by famous by musical theatre legends George Hearn and Angela Lansbury, and made even more famous by the Tim Burton movie starring Johnny Depp and Helena Bonham Carter.

Patrons were encouraged to dress up in Victorian England themed clothing while employees dressed as the various characters from the musical. Playing on the television screen was, you guessed it, the Tim Burton movie adaptation of the musical. As patrons got their shaves by a man dressed as the sinister Sweeny Todd, meat pies were served hot out of a small oven. Patrons and staff sang along to the various songs. It was creepy and weird, and I *loved* it. *Sweeny Todd* ranks on the top of my list of favorite musicals, and it was one of the most memorable experiences I can recall in recent times. I had no problem handing over $50 for a memorable experience that happened to come with a haircut and a shave.

Creating Unforgettable Moments for Customers

Kimpton Hotels is notorious for creating "Kimpton moments" with its guests. What is a Kimpton moment? "It's a ridiculously personal experience between you and another person."[9] What do these moments involve? Director of Social Media Whitney Smith explains:

> Turns out, it's a rather simple formula — as many great ones are. Throughout the day, no matter where you are: at a physical location, on social media, over the phone, via email etc., Kimpton is going to do all they can to appreciate you.[10]

According to the hotel chain, the magic behind making these moments possible is not difficult. "A team of social agents monitor the social web almost 24 hours a day, 7 days a week assisting customers, posting content, and looking for potential opportunities. Next, when a potential moment is found, the social team gathers as much information as they can without prying. Finally, the opportunity is then routed down to the property level where the property takes the contextual information provided and comes up with the ridiculously personal experiences that many guests encounter."[11]

Take for instance when a guest sent a social media message to the hotel asking if they were able to get the AMC channel on the room television. He didn't want to miss the series finale of Breaking Bad. While they were not able to accommodate the initial request, the hotel staff was empowered and enabled to make a reservation for the guest at a local bar that was hosting a watch party. As the guest was out, a personal Walter White amenity was delivered to the guest's room, "rock" candy included.[12]

Creating moments is similar to seeing something in a store that reminds you of someone special. You say to yourself, "I think they would really like this." You just get it for them, regardless of the time of year. It does not have to be their birthday or Christmas. You just knew it would make them happy. This is how simple creating memorable experiences can be for your customers. It's thinking outside the box and empowering your employees to brainstorm and use their creativity to come with ideas that will make the customer smile. It does not have to be a special occasion; it rather should be the normal practice of your business to make these experiences happen.

Located less than an hour from Salt Lake City is the outdoor resort town of Park City. It is home to the world-famous Sundance film festival and many celebrity homes. During the off-season, which is defined as April-October, the local resorts give impressive discounts and hotel packages to Utah residents to fill rooms. I decided to take advantage and booked a room at the Waldorf Astoria. The presidential suite rate was the same as a normal room rate and included a personal butler and breakfast for two. It was a great offer and a chance to get away for the evening. I took a friend and we indulged in the good life for a night. During my brief stay, my butler went above and beyond to take care of me. We discussed how I enjoy collecting foreign currency as a hobby. He personally unfolded and re-folded my clothes upon checkout. Without asking, after returning from dinner, a beautiful display of chamomile teas with a handwritten note asking me to enjoy a good night's sleep awaited me on a turned down bed. At check out, the receptionist handed me an envelope with a piece of foreign currency. It was from my butler, and yet another note explaining that he had been on a recent trip and wanted me to have it for my collection. I was touched by this exemplary act of service, and I have that piece of currency in my collection to this day. He used the knowledge I provided him to create a memorable experience with a touch of personality.

Bottom Line: Give customers a reason to come back. If your customers only come once, then your business will close as fast as it opened. Brand loyalty is crucial in this new era of doing business. Customers can get a product or service anywhere. Make sure they are coming to *your* business each time. Say yes to them, make sure they are taken care of, and that you convey your appreciation for their business. Don't be afraid to get creative! In this era where everyone sells a similar product or service, make yours stand out. Empower employees to work together to create unforgettable moments for customers.

Chapter 7

Customer Service & Country Music

"Always do more than is expected of you." – Gen. George Patton

HARLAN HOWARD ONCE SAID that country music was nothing more than "three chords and the truth. It talked about true life; the music was a simple plea."¹

Country music used to be uncomplicated, direct and to the point. It passionately conveyed the dreams and hopes of the working American. It represented a time when morality and values meant more than making money. It was about hard-working cowboys. It was about passionate lovers. It was about Jesus and blue jeans. It was the music of a time when a handshake was a binding legal contract, and when a man's word was his bond.

But now, country music has changed. It is like when we were kids and wanted to make breakfast in bed for our parents. We went to the refrigerator and took a little of this and a little of that and threw it all together, resulting in a disgusting concoction.

Dare I say that modern country music has followed the same recipe for disaster? It is an infusion of pop, alternative, and even contemporary Christian worship. You see rap artists doing covers of the great country classics. It has evolved from Wrangler jeans to khaki pants, from cowboy boots to tennis shoes. Today's country music has *some* elements of its historic past. But just because a song has a fiddle and a steel guitar does not make it authentically country. Most diehard country fans can see right through the fakeness, the gaudiness and the hysteria. Maybe that's why I love the movie *Pure Country*. George Strait, the uncontested king of country music, made this movie in the 1990's about a famous country music singer who sold out to the pressures of the industry. His manager was more focused on making money than music. Finally, frustration caught up to Strait's character. The two have a showdown of sorts and Strait draws a line, stating that his show will now consist of him and his guitar. No sets. No lights. No smoke machines or crazy special effects. He wanted to get back to basics.

Consumers can see through the fakeness when you put good service up against the purported standards of today. I think we would do well to go back to traditional service values that made business great. Companies spend millions a year in research to tell them what customers are thinking. And you know what? They all say the same thing: customers value genuine experiences six days of the week and twice on Sunday. There is a benefit to every product, and some are better than others. But people will stay loyal to a brand if they can be assured of the experience that accompanies it. They go hand-in-hand, like the strings on a banjo.

It is sad how terms and conditions have replaced a handshake. Pre-screening algorithms now do the hiring versus a real conversation with a human being. Now, I get it. We live in a growing and changing world. Technology has changed how we do things. In many ways, this has changed our lives for the better. But we must not abandon the time-tested values that made business great. Honesty, appreciation, and authenticity will always win over mobile apps, dot com convenience and discounts.

Companies now perform standardized routines which fall under the umbrellas of customer service but is far from the actual execution of it. I am in no way saying every organization performs this way. There are still wonderful customer focused organizations out there. Rather, I am expressing an opinion that I feel reflects that of most consumers. Companies now just go through the motions. They deliver a transactional interaction, moving from one customer to the next like drones on an assembly line.

At the beginning of this chapter, I mentioned the movie *Pure Country*. In one scene, George Strait's character goes back to his small Texas hometown. He walks into a diner with a few old cowboys and a friendly waitress. She offers him a cup of coffee and a piece of pie, and with a smile on her face says, "Welcome". When I think of this scene, I reflect upon how simple customer service can be. There are no flashy gimmicks or clever marketing schemes; just great service delivered by a genuine person. This level of customer interaction speaks volumes to me versus the options today. I know my opinion will not resonate with everyone. Yes, it is nice to sit back on your couch and order your groceries from home. It is convenient to order something in the morning and have it delivered by the afternoon. These are great conveniences, but they don't provide memorable experiences.

There is a very large credit union operating who at the time of this writing currently holds my car loan. I chose this institution because of the interest rate. Had I known then what I know now, I would have gladly paid a little more to get better service elsewhere.

This credit union has made it a practice to have as *little* customer interaction as possible. The branch phone numbers don't direct you to the local office, but rather to the larger national call center. The average wait time for this organization is fourteen minutes. Yes, you heard me right: fourteen excruciating minutes is the *average*. If someone from the actual credit union fails to pick up the phone, customers are rerouted to a third-party call center to help with overflow. This third-party company however does not have access customer accounts and cannot provide any real assistance. The sole purpose of this secondary call center is to tell already frustrated customers to keep waiting. When I think of this company, a face palm to the forehead usually follows. This is an example of the new face of customer service. And like new country music, it is just downright awful.

Keep It Simple

There is no magic formula or complex set of procedures that govern customer service. It is, in reality, very simple. It is about taking care of customers and creating an experience that begs them to return. KPI metrics and surveys fail to convey what simple acts of service mean to customers. If you want to create customers for life, provide an experience they will never forget. It's not brain surgery here.

Not only must it be memorable, but also consistent. Customers get frustrated when they don't have consistency across an organization. If I visit a store in one city and have a great service experience, and then visit that same brand location in another city and receive terrible service, what message is being sent to the customer? It screams discriminatory service. Now, I don't mean discriminatory in the traditional sense. No one should ever be discriminated against for any reason. What I am saying is that when an organization picks and chooses when it wants to provide good service, that can be considered discriminatory service. Why should customers be treated any different simply based off the location they are in or because of different circumstances? If I stay at a luxury hotel in New York, should my experience be any different at the same brand in Seattle?

I will say it again: providing good service is hard work. It takes a lot to be consistent. But you are either in it for the long haul or not. It can't be a back and forth practice. And for those who doubt that this level of consistency can be practiced at large enterprise-wide organizations, I ask you to re-think that belief. Disney, Ritz-Carlton, Four Seasons, Zappos and Nordstrom are just a few of the many large organizations who follow a consistent set of standards around the world. When I visit any of these properties, stores or amusement parks, I know what to expect. Things are going to happen, and mistakes will be made. People are human, after all. But customers have come to expect and even demand a certain level of consistency at organizations. Herve Humler, President of Ritz-Carlton Hotels, states that within his organization every department has three daily lineups during major shift changes to reinforce the company's value system. He states:

> It is my job to daily remind ourselves and those who work for us that we are not in the business of selling hotel rooms. We are in the business of providing exceptional service. This is the reason we conduct

a lineup three times per day, every day, all over the world. We remind our Ladies and Gentlemen daily about what is important to our customers. Energizing a workforce has to be a daily commitment. We pledge to commit ourselves to deliver excellence to our guests every day. Not whenever we want, but always.[2]

Shortly before the final publication of this book, I went to a store that sold western apparel at our outlet mall. Being close to Christmas, I could not pass up the sales being offered. This store was also brand new to our outlet mall. They had only been open a few days. I purchased several shirts and socks that had a red tag on them, which meant the sale price was final and no returns were allowed. As I walked out of the store, I noticed the cowboy boots were being sold for a ridiculously low price and I wanted to buy a pair. I left the store thinking I should have used the money I spent on the shirts for the boots instead. The next day, I decided I wanted to buy the boots. The receipt did not expressly say that my items could not be *exchanged*, so I took a chance. I was honestly expecting the worst. After all, consumers have come to expect that. Saying yes to the customer is out of the vernacular for most organizations. Why should this one be any different?

I entered the store and saw the associate who helped me the day prior. For the sake of this story, I will call her Janet. She was friendly and welcomed me back. I explained my situation and asked if I could exchange the red tag items as a credit toward the boots. Gearing up to hear that dreaded word "unfortunately", what happened next was a complete surprise: Janet said it was no problem to exchange the items. I picked my jaw up off the ground and explained to her that I was not expecting to be treated right.

Janet's demeanor and professionalism proved to me that she is passionate about service and recognizes the power a customer has. I struck up a conversation with her about how strongly I feel about customer service, and she conveyed the same feeling. To her, it all came down to treating others how she would want to be treated. It was as if this associate jumped into my computer and read this book ahead of time. It was a perfect execution of all the principles I have shared. And to make this experience even better than it already was, she marked the boots down an additional twenty percent. That is what sold me right then and there, and I knew I would be a customer for life. She wanted me to know that I was welcome to come back to her place of business through her actions and the experience she created.

Christina McKinney was a guest at the beautiful Gaylord Opryland Hotel in Nashville for a conference. She was entranced by the clock in her hotel room which played soothing spa sounds throughout the night. She wanted this clock for her home. She decided to send a Twitter message to the hotel asking for the name of the company who made the clock. The hotel responded that the clocks were custom made and were not available for the general public. Saddened, McKinney resumed her time at the conference. She went out to dinner with fellow conference attendees when she received the shock of her life. Upon returning to her room, Christina saw a new hotel clock sitting on her bed with a note from the staff thanking her for being a valued guest. The note read that they hoped she would enjoy the soothing spa sounds at home. This simple gesture made Christina a customer for life. Gaylord Opryland recognized an opportunity to provide an amazing customer experience, and it paid off. Soon, everyone at the conference was talking about what the hotel had done.[3] I personally would come to expect nothing less from the good people of Nashville, my beautiful hometown!

These two stories demonstrate how simple customer service can create loyalty to a brand. What is your organization doing to create this kind of brand loyalty? Are you giving customers a reason to recommend your business to my family and friends, or a reason to stay away and advise others to do the same?

Take Pride in your Work

Employees can't have pride in their work when an organization places no trust in them. How can anyone feel a sense of accomplishment when they have been deprived of innovation and creativity? I speak from experience that there is no greater feeling in the world than a sense of triumph from going above and beyond. I can look back and say that the outcome was because of me; no managers, no committee approval, no red tape. It was all because of *me*. Some may think that I am boasting about this, but there is a major difference in being prideful and proud. Being prideful is exercising a spirit of self-indulgent conceit that elevates you above others. Being proud, however, is simply taking a moment to step back and reflect on a job well done.

In the 1990's, country music superstar Aaron Tippin sang, "When the quittin' whistle blows and the dust settles down, there ain't no trophies or cheering crowds. You'll face yourself at the end of the day and be damned proud of whatever you've made. Can't hang it on the wall for the world to see, but you've got yourself a Working Man's Ph.D." [4]

I was honored to receive a major award which I felt was undeserved for simply doing my job. I assisted newly married clients with a home equity loan. They were referred to my branch after having a less than positive experience with the bank's call center. I apologized for the bad experience and was determined to make things right. The young couple explained they needed funds to complete some landscaping projects for their new home. But they had a small baby, and it was difficult for them to drive the twenty miles to the office. As a result, we did everything by phone. I took their applications, got the loan approved, ordered title work and set a closing date. Despite their best efforts, they informed me they were not able to arrange a babysitter for the closing. I decided to leave the branch early and drive to their home. They were beyond grateful and continually praised me for coming to them and accommodating their busy schedules. I thought nothing of it. I was simply doing my job. I was notified some weeks later that those same clients had contacted the Office of the President and shared this story, and I was given the prestigious award.

I do not share this story to boast. Rather, I share it because I am proud of it. The award looks nice on a resume and shines nicely on a desk. But I am not proud of the award; I am proud of how I earned it. I want others to know that feeling. I am thankful that I was able to get the job done and take care of my customers. I sincerely wish companies would empower their employees with the ability to create these opportunities. Like the song says, I was incredibly proud of what I accomplished that day, and I carry that feeling with me when things get difficult in my professional life. I have been proud of my employees when they have gone above and beyond to make memorable experiences for customers. Not only am I proud of them, but I am proud of myself for teaching them to do things without my supervision. Those positive feelings make you want to come to work and serve people. When you empower employees with the ability to make amazing things happen for customers, I promise you the results will far exceed anything that can be measured on a customer survey or meaningless metric report.

Love What You Do

The most employee friendly culture will be ineffective if one is not passionate about their work. Regardless of how you feel about him politically, President Donald Trump really drives home this point. In his book *Think Big*, Mr. Trump tells the story of a good friend who worked in the stock market. He made a lot of money and was very successful. However, he was miserable. His wife made it very clear that if the income ever diminished, she would leave him. His father owned the stock brokerage firm and was emotionally and professionally abusive.

One day, this man was asked to spearhead a project renovating a golf course at a club Mr. Trump happened to be a member of. The man found that he had a passion for landscape design. The man asked Mr. Trump for advice, and he offered the following:

> You have to love what you do, or you are never going to be successful, no matter what you do in life. If you love what you do, you're going to work harder, you're going to try harder, you're going to be better at it, and you're going to enjoy life a lot more.[5]

And with that, the man resigned from his father's business. His wife left him. He started his own landscape design and real estate consulting business. He was making hundreds of thousands of dollars less. And you know what? He could not have been happier. Adults will spend on average most of their lives at a place of employment. That old saying of "If you love what you do, then you never work a day in your life" is completely true.

Companies like Zappos have created a culture where their employees love to come to work. They love it so much that they are paid to quit if they are not happy. Of their entire workforce, only 12 percent of Zappos employees end up resigning and taking the money.[6] The vast majority love what they do and where they work. They are proud to say they work at Zappos. Amazon followed suit with a "Pay to Leave" program.[7] Giving employees opportunities to be proud of their work people is a good thing; embrace it!

Bottom line: Customer service is simple and to the point. People today are more socially aware than ever before. They can see when something is fake and lacks real genuineness. Employees want to be proud of what they do; give them a reason to be! Empower and trust them, and they will shine for you! When they love what they do and where they work, amazing experiences will happen for your customers!

Chapter 8

Accountability: Working Together for the Good of the Customer

"Every employee can affect your company's brand, not just the front-line employees that are paid to talk to your customers."
– Tony Hsieh

I READ A STORY that says:

There were four people named Everybody, Somebody, Anybody, and Nobody. There was an important job to be done and Everybody was asked to do it. Everybody was sure Somebody would do it. Anybody could have done it, but Nobody did it. Somebody got angry about that, because it was Everybody's job. Everybody thought Anybody could do it but Nobody realized that Everybody wouldn't do it. It ended up that Everybody blamed Somebody when Nobody did what Anybody could have done.[1]

Accountability is creating a culture among employees that tells customers their business matters. It is entrusting employees to do the right thing each time and being responsible for their business actions and decisions. It is the willingness to show your customers that you really do care about them and uphold an organization wide pledge to respond to customer issues as they arrive.

Customers do not care which department they reach when they are seeking help. They just want their problem solved! It should be the mantra of every organization to simply make it happen, regardless of the department called. The end goal is to bring a satisfactory result to the customer. When organizations do not entrust teams to work together, they can't give personalized service. This frustrates both employees and customers. According to Saleforce, 78% of consumers have ended a business relationship due to bad service, and specifically a company failing to work together to correct a negative situation.[2] Corporate culture needs to include being accountable for the actions of the entire team. If you want to drive your customers away in droves, make sure to pass their concern on from department to department with a "not my problem" mindset. Put up barriers and obstacles for your customers that drag out their negative experience as long as possible. That will guarantee your customers *don't* return! However, if you want to keep customers coming back, enable employees to act and make the situation right.

It's Not My Fault

I had a horrible experience at a local car wash. This business used to be locally owned and prided itself on providing personalized customer service. I enjoyed going to this business quite often. The attendants would go above and beyond to make sure my vehicle was clean. The lobby was welcoming with complimentary soft drinks, coffee and water. But then, things took a dramatic turn. This company was purchased by a mega-corporation. Online customer reviews plummeted. The lobby was completely transformed into a bland waiting space. The complimentary beverages were removed and replaced with soda machines. Attendants were now instructed to clean out the cars in less than five minutes to push more into the cleaning bay. The lack of care and quality was apparent. Instead of having a beautifully cleaned car, attendants are forced to rush and often leave behind large amounts of dirt, crumbs and other debris that are clearly noticed upon returning to their vehicles.

I visited the car wash in January 2020 because I had received a gift card there. I generally take my vehicle to a competitor where customers can clean out their own vehicle with vacuum hoses. It is a no-frills car wash, but the lower cost is well worth it. Having this gift card in hand, I tried this location again. I would give them the benefit of the doubt, hoping conditions had changed. Sadly, I was mistaken.

I had a 2001 Dodge Ram truck with black fender flares. Upon exiting the car wash, I heard a disturbing sound from the passenger side. I climbed out and noticed that one of the flares was shredded. I immediately hailed a manager who took an incident report. I was informed that I would be contacted within 24 hours by a general manager. A day later, I received a call and within only a few words, I could tell this manager wanted a fight. Without providing any evidence to the contrary, he informed me that the car wash would not be replacing the damaged item due to the flare being supposedly damaged previously. I was confident there was no previous damage to the vehicle and asserted that the truck was not damaged when it entered the car wash. Suddenly upon exiting, there was a broken piece of my vehicle in their wash bay. This was a very simple issue that should have been met with an apology, followed by an effort to get the piece repaired or replaced. The cost of the item was less than one hundred dollars. It was not a major issue. But this manager made it into a dramatic spectacle. He was rude and condescending. He maintained that he had pictures of the previous damage yet refused to provide them. I was not allowed to speak to any managers above him, citing company policy which forbids customers to have access to district or regional managers. This manager bragged about how many complaints he received from customers daily, and how often his district manager was called. I thought to myself, *I can certainly see why you have so many complaints!*

The company eventually took care of the problem, but it was a horrific experience that made me never want to do business with them again, gift card or not. He even had the audacity to continue to suggest it was my fault with a condescending email. It stated, in short, that I had to admit the vehicle was damaged for it to be fixed. The nerve of this guy! He wanted to keep drilling it in that I somehow was at fault, taunting me as if I was making some outlandish request for the damage to be fixed. This email response reinforced that the only concern of this manager and company was profit. Rather than correct a clear mistake on their part, they wanted to fight me for every nickel and dime. They made up their mind before doing any investigation that I was wrong and they were right, despite the broken piece of my vehicle being retrieved in their wash bay. This manager clearly does not possess basic leadership or customer service centric skills. A good manager knows that you *never* blame the customer for the problem. You listen, empathize, and make things right. Had this company promoted a spirit of accountability, then I suspect the experience would have been far better. Now, I will forever associate this brand with feelings of negativity rather than gratification.

Just the opposite occurred to a good friend of mine. He had a situation with the online retailer Amazon in which they took accountability for a problem. My friend had ordered an item and for whatever reason he received another person's order. He contacted the online giant. Rather than make excuses, Amazon took accountability for the problem. Not only did they rush ship the correct items to my friend and the other shopper, but they told my friend to keep the first mis-delivered item. He was so happy to receive a free space heater!

Amazon displays real accountability: resolving issues regardless of who was at fault. Organizations must enable employees to allow customers to be treated right and have their concerns addressed and remedied. They require the ability to take care of a problem even if it means having to reach out to third parties, additional vendors, or take a loss. The values, norms, beliefs and practices of an organization must be focused on serving the customer. A recipe for disaster is almost certain if this is not the case. Administrative staff, supervisors, middle managers, and even top executives are accountable to the customer.

I told a story earlier about a large automotive banking institution that personified this kind of culture. I shared the details of how it took over seventeen minutes to reach an employee to achieve a task that took thirty seconds to perform. The only person who suffered was the customer, who had to wait for this unnecessary amount of time, which in turn created a negative experience. This financial organization lived the "not my problem" mentality to the letter. What they and others fail to realize is that way of thinking is a stake through the heart of customer service. These misguided cultures promote a belief that because an employee does not have direct contact with the customer, the concerns of the customer are not relevant. An organization with a culture that teaches employees to lose the sense of being connected to the customer fails to see their indifference mindset hurts the customer experience. The correct mindset should be, "It's somebody else's job to take care of the customer directly, and it's my job to support and assist that individual to make the customer experience the best it can be."

Six Reasons for a Culture Void of Accountability

I have found throughout my career six key reasons companies fail to promote a culture of accountability:

1. Service excellence is not at the heart of the organization. Consistent high standards are not the defining aspect of a company, but rather just the product or service being offered. A company says in their mission statement how important treating customers is, but in reality, it's nothing more than lip service. This is dangerous for any organization. Gordon Ramsey constantly shouts, "Standards! Where are your standards?" on his cooking programs. Ramsey understands the importance of maintaining a consistent set of high standards, and he goes crazy when they are broken.
2. Many companies think the senior executives should dictate the customer experience. Rather, they have failed to realize that it is the *customer* who has the power to keep the doors open or expeditiously close them. Customers are telling companies what they have come to expect through their spending habits, surveys, and social media posts. But are the people in charge listening? Customers expect excellence

every time; organizations deliver mediocrity most of the time. Your customers are telling you loud and clear what they are expecting.

3. The organization thinks the only important interaction takes place is at the point of sale. They believe the product/service speaks for itself and is customer intimate. This could not be further from the truth. What good is a customer buying a product if they are made to feel horrible for doing so? I know I would much rather spend my hard-earned money at a company who values my business versus a cultureless big-box shop for a slight discount.

4. Customer facing staff does not feel fully supported by the organization, which in turn negatively affects the customer experience. At the risk of sounding repetitive, if every member of the organization does not have a customer driven mindset, failure is sure to follow. Back office and non-customer facing employees often fall into that "not my problem" mindset when things go wrong. They feel because they do not have to face the customer directly, their problems are not of major concern. Every employee needs to remember who keeps the company in business, and who pays those paychecks every two weeks. Contrary to belief, your HR department *does not* pay you; the *customer* does.

5. Non-customer facing staff and management don't regard themselves as being in the customer service business. I know for myself when I had to deal with back-office departments at major financial institutions, this was a notorious problem. "I just prepare documents" or "I work in compliance" was often the response I would get when trying to solve customer problems. These employees, departments and office cultures

do not believe in the customer first mindset. Yes, they are not directly answering to the customer. But I *am*! And it is that customer who is paying my salary and that of every employee at that organization. Every employee should that mindset.

6. The organization's systems and procedures are not conducive to service excellence. They are more focused on internal drivers such as metrics and KPI's (key performance indicators). When you bind employees to a set of metrics, performance suffers. I am not saying that employee productivity should not be tracked; I am saying is that every customer situation is *unique*. What works for one customer may not work for another. Employees need freedom to take care of customers without having to live within an unrealistic set of metrics. Zappos, the online shoe retailer, is obsessed with service. They have created a culture that throws all the traditional call center norms out the window. The only metric Zappos cares about is customer satisfaction. In 2016, employee Steven Weinstein took a call that lasted over ten hours. That one call set the world record for the longest customer service interaction in history. Other organizations would have chastised this employee for not staying within a set of guidelines that benefit the internal drivers. But not Zappos! He became a customer service rock-star across the internet.[3]

The Customer Is Not Always Right

Wait, in a book focused on providing outstanding customer service, you're saying that the customer is not always right?

Yes, I am.

You can't please everyone. This is especially true of customers. "The customer is always right" was a slogan coined by Marshall Field, who combined it with, "Give the lady what she wants." At his Chicago department store, he believed that customers should be treated seriously. But what happens if customers are dishonest and have unrealistic expectations?

There are some customers who will never appreciate anything you do. This is not a reflection on you, however. It is part of a deeper problem within that individual. There are some people who have been so emotionally hurt that they have forgotten how to find joy in anything. They have lost all sense of reality because they are so blinded by emotional trauma. My heart goes out to these people because I have been there. I struggle with deep and often debilitating depression and anxiety. I have struggled with severe suicidal tendencies. But I also will not allow customers like this to manipulate situations to their advantage, and neither should you. I will also never tolerate abuse of employees no matter the situation. I will take full accountability for a situation and do everything in my power to make it right. But if a customer does not want to accept what I am offering, that decision is theirs. The belief that "the customer is always right" is about as outdated as a 1950's television set. I use the following analogy to explain this logic: Ranchers will place hay bales in the fields for the cows to come eat. For whatever reason, there will always be a few stubborn ones who refuse what is being offered. The primary role of an organization is to create the best experience possible for each customer. The choice to accept that service, however, is entirely up to them.

The problem with this belief is that it leads to widespread abuse of resources and employees. As I have said before, some people are just mean. They have deep emotional issues and need a lot of help, which is outside of your role as a business owner. I will repeat myself from before: my heart goes out to these people who suffer, and I will do all in my power to assist and get them help. But I will *never* allow my employees or other customers to be abused and taken advantage of. Good managers will step up and defend their employees, even if it means a loss for the company. The Ritz-Carlton's vice-president of global marketing, Lisa Holladay, expounds on this thought:

> I have watched our general managers stand up for our Ladies and Gentlemen over very high profile, high paying guests that were being inappropriate with our hotel staff. I watched them put our Ladies and Gentlemen *first*.[4]

Will this result in a loss of revenue from these customers? Yes. But as a business, you must ask yourself if that is the kind of customer you really want in the first place. Your employees will begin to view you with disdain as you let them be abused and berated. Customers will attempt to take advantage of your business. This cannot happen and must be avoided. I recognize that companies have established anti-customer policies and practices. But I am also not blind to reality. While we would hope that the world is full of good people, sometimes human beings are not the best they can be. We live in a world where defrauding and scamming others is a common practice. As a banking professional, I saw this daily. Strive to be hospitable, but exercise caution. If customers know they can take advantage of you, they will look for every opportunity to do so.

Regardless of the industry I am in, I make it a personal goal to deliver the best experience possible for my guests. I live my life by a code of honesty and integrity. I will not lie or deceive my guests to make a quick profit. I am not saying this makes me better than others.

The Customer Service Revolution

I just have a code of ethics that govern how I live. That said, I also will not allow customers to take advantage of me.

As an auto finance manager, I was contacted on a Saturday about a vehicle I had for sale. Being an eight-year-old car, it was in very good shape. There were some small cosmetic dings and dents, but that is to be expected. However, it had low mileage and ran great. I was contacted by a woman who lived four hours away in another state. I was completely honest and stated that I had personally test driven the car and I was not aware of any issues. It was a clean title vehicle and had a good service history. A third-party mechanic inspected it and it passed. The woman begged me to come in on my day off and outside of our normal days of operation. I wanted her to be happy, so I agreed to meet her. She drove the vehicle and was pleased with it. She declined putting an extended warranty on the vehicle. I finalized the sale and she drove away happy. Two hours later, she called on my personal cell phone and became hostile. She claimed the vehicle "blew up" as she left and that I needed to refund her money. I attempted to diagnose the issue, but she refused. I directed her to a dealership a mile away from her and offered to pay for a diagnostic, and she refused. I advised her to use the powertrain warranty we place on all used cars, and she refused. This woman wanted a full refund, no questions asked. I consulted with the dealership owner and we agreed that unwinding the deal was the best option for this woman. I profusely apologized for her experience. I explained that I would refund her money within two days. I offered to refund her for the gas she put in the vehicle after purchase. But none of this was good enough. This woman began making outrageous demands. She stated that I needed to reimburse all her fuel coming to the dealership. She stated that I needed to compensate her for a day of travel, and for her being inconvenienced. The list read on like a list of charges on *The Peoples Court*. Everything I said was met with intimidation from this customer, and I had to politely but firmly establish that I had done my part. I was not going to kowtow to the outrageous demands of an understandably frustrated customer.

This woman at no time thanked me for coming in on my day off. She cursed at me. She called me a liar and a cheater. I am none of those things. Anyone who knows me will confirm that. I did not force this woman to drive four hours to buy a car. I did however rearrange my schedule on my personal time off to extend the best service possible, and I took accountability for the problem and tried to make it right. But with this customer, I could have refunded her two times over and she still would have found things to be angry about. I can't please everyone, and neither can you. Having a customer focused mindset will not always produce happy outcomes. Rather, a service mindset is about providing consistency. That guest to me was no different than any other. I did for her what I would do for any other. The fact that she did not respond in kind was no reflection on my service execution. You cannot blame yourself or your employees for having an upset customer. A true customer service recovery failure is when you do *nothing* to appease the guest and make things right. But when a customer doesn't accept your service, move onto the next one. You were consistent, and that's what matters.

Bottom line: Taking care of the customer is the responsibility of every employee. Regardless of position within the company, the customer is the sole purpose for the organization being in existence. Without customers, there is no revenue. No revenue, no paychecks. Companies need to establish a customer first mindset and enable their employees to be able to work together or even independently, to resolve customer concerns. When situations do happen and customers are upset, do not pass responsibility from one department to another. Take ownership and do everything to make it right.

Afterword

CUSTOMER SERVICE IS ABOUT taking risks, throwing out the ideas that didn't work and keeping what did. I am not suggesting that you do everything I have spoken about to produce great customer service. These are tools for your use. You can use one of them, all of them, or none of them. You may even disagree with what I have to say. That is perfectly fine! These are my stories and opinions which happen to coincide with industry expertise and that have worked for me throughout my career.

I will leave you with what I feel are the key points from this book:

1. Respect the power a customer has
2. Genuinely welcome your customers
3. Give them a reason to come back
4. Good service begins with good employees; treat them right
5. Be consistent in your service delivery
6. Keep it simple, but don't be afraid to get creative
7. Empower employees and they will produce great results
8. Give your employees a reason to be proud of their work
9. Be accountable for mistakes and correct them

And so, here we are. I hope you have enjoyed this book. It has been a labor of love. There is one single message I have tried to convey, and it is this: treat people right, be good to each other and live the golden rule. These basic lessons are what we learned watching Mr. Rogers Neighborhood as kids. It is not groundbreaking science, but in today's business world, is sadly has become a revolutionary concept. While companies are so concerned about the bottom line, they should be more concerned about what will happen when customers choose to take their business elsewhere. No organization is too big to fail. Customers have real power to control the destiny of an organization, and they are not afraid to exercise it.

Holding it all together are employees. They are the most vital equation. Without them, everything I have said about service is irrelevant. If there are no employees, nothing happens! My hope is that no one ever experiences what I did: being professionally dehumanized to the point of suicide. I would not wish that experience upon my worst enemy. People are people. Not everyone is loving and kind. Some people are incredibly evil. I know that all too well. But kindness and dignity are asked of all of us, and we should strive to do our part.

I close with the words of UCLA basketball coach and hall of famer John Wooden: "Respect a man, and he will do all the more."[1]

Endnotes

Preface

1. "Definition of revolution," as accessed in 2019 via https://www.merriam-webster.com/dictionary/revolution

Chapter 1

1. Jessica Schiffer, "The Fascinating Psychology Behind Buyer's Remorse," https://www.whowhatwear.com/why-we-get-buyers-remorse

2. Michael Solomon, *The Heart of Hospitality: Great Hotel and Restaurant Leaders Share Their Secrets* (New York City, NY: Select Books, 2016)

3. Greg Ciotti, "7 Times Excellent Customer Service Was Delivered Over Email," 2019, https://www.helpscout.com/helpu/excellent-customer-service/

Chapter 2

1. Hawaiian 2013 Revised Statutes, TITLE I, General Provisions 5-7.5, https://www.capitol.hawaii.gov/hrscurrent/Vol01_Ch0001-0042F/HRS0005/HRS_0005-0007_0005.htm, 2019

2. Pat Eggleton, "Prego—A useful word," 2010, https://www.italymagazine.com/featured-story/prego-useful-word

3. Theodore Kinni, *Be Our Guest—Perfecting the Art of Customer Service* (Los Angeles, CA: Disney Book Group, 2011)

4. Sarah Boutin, "Behind the scenes at Salesforce.com: our aloha spirit," 2019, https://www.salesforce.com/blog/2014/07/behind-the-scenes-at-salesforcecom-our-aloha-spirit.html

5. Theodore Kinni, *Be Our Guest—Perfecting the Art of Customer Service* (Los Angeles, CA: Disney Book Group, 2011)

Chapter 3

1. Martha Finney, "How do you keep your sense of humanity in HR?" 2018, https://hrexecutive.com/how-do-you-keep-your-sense-of-\humanity-in-hr/

2. Lauren McDonald, Personal Post, 2020, https://www.linkedin.com/in/laurenmcdonaldgogogo/

3. Amanda Woods, "US Bank employee fired for giving $20 to struggling customer", https://nypost.com/2020/01/17/us-bank-employee-fired-for-giving-20-to-struggling-customer/

4. Maribeth Bisinere, "Eight key takeaways from the 2019 Disney Institute", https://www.disneyinstitute.com/blog/eight-keytakeaways-from-the-2019-disney-institute-customer-experiencesummit/

5. President John F Kennedy, as quoted from an address to the American University of Washington, DC, 1963, http://www.jfklibrary.org/archives/other-resources/john-f-kennedy-speeches/american-university-19630610

Chapter 4

1. Julia Fenton, "No magic formula for culture," 2017, https://www.businesshorsepower.com/no-magic-formula-culture/

2. Muriel Wilkins, "Signs that you're a micromanager", 2014, https://hbr.org/2014/11/signs-that-youre-a-micromanager

3. Conan O'Brien, "Address to Dartmouth College Graduates," 2011, https://www.dartmouth.edu/~commence/news/speeches/2011/obrien-speech.html

4. Adam Toporek, "The Ritz-Carlton's Famous $2000 Rule," 2012, https://customersthatstick.com/blog/customer-loyalty/the-ritz-carltons-famous-2000-rule/

5. Neil Patel, "Tony Hsieh, Zappos, and the Art of Great Company Culture," 2019, https://neilpatel.com/blog/zappos-art-of-culture/

6. Michele Chandler, "Happiness leads to profits," 2010, https://www.gsb.stanford.edu/insights/tony-hsieh-happiness-leads-profits

7. Marc Solow, "Culture and engagement," 2015, https://www2.deloitte.com/us/en/insights/focus/human-capital-trends/2015/employee-engagement-culture-human-capital-trends-2015.html

8. Dale Buss, "The power of employee engagement," 2013, https://www.shrm.org/resourcesandtools/hr-topics/employeerelations/pages/power-of-employee-engagement.aspx

9. Neil Patel, "Tony Hsieh, Zappos, and the Art of Great Company Culture," 2019, https://neilpatel.com/blog/zappos-art-of-culture/

10. Michael Solomon, *The Heart of Hospitality: Great Hotel and Restaurant Leaders Share Their Secrets* (New York City, NY: Select Books, 2016)

Chapter 5

1. Phantom of the Opera Facts, https://www.thephantomoftheopera.com/facts-figures/

2. Theodore Kinni, *Be Our Guest—Perfecting the Art of Customer Service* (Los Angeles, CA: Disney Book Group, 2011)

3. Oracle, "Smarter CX", 2020, https://smartercx.com/customer-service-vs-customer-experience-whats-the-difference/

4. John Nemo, "What a NASA janitor can teach us about living a better life," 2014, https://www.bizjournals.com/bizjournals/how-to/growth-strategies/2014/12/what-a-nasa-janitor-can-teach-us.html

5. Michael Solomon, *The Heart of Hospitality: Great Hotel and Restaurant Leaders Share Their Secrets* (New York City, NY: Select Books, 2016)

6. Ibid

7. Ibid

8. KSL TV, 2014, https://www.ksl.com/article/32695864/stylist-shares-secret-of-why-food-in-ads-looks-so-good

9. http://cinema.com/articles/463/shrek-production-information.phtml

10. Theodore Kinni, *Be Our Guest—Perfecting the Art of Customer Service* (Los Angeles, CA: Disney Book Group, 2011)

11. Michael Solomon, *The Heart of Hospitality: Great Hotel and Restaurant Leaders Share Their Secrets* (New York City, NY: Select Books, 2016).

12. Theodore Kinni, *Be Our Guest—Perfecting the Art of Customer Service* (Los Angeles, CA: Disney Book Group, 2011).

13. Ibid.

14. Stephen Hyken, "Customer experience is the new brand", https://www.forbes.com/sites/shephyken/2018/07/15/customer-experience-is-the-new-brand/#23ada08e7f52

15. Toma Kulbyte, "37 Customer Experience Statistics You Need to Know for 2020", 2020, https://www.superoffice.com/blog/customer-experience-statistics/

16. Sweor, "27 Eye Opening Website Statistics: Is your website costing you clients?", 2019 https://www.sweor.com/firstimpressions

17. Toma Kulbyte, "37 Customer Experience Statistics You Need to Know for 2020", 2020, https://www.superoffice.com/blog/customer-experience-statistics/

18. Nichols Cole, "The Power Of Live Chat: 5 Surprising Statistics That Show How Consumers Want Their Questions Answered", https://www.inc.com/nicolas-cole/the-power-of-live-chat-5-surprising-statistics-that-show-how-consumers-want-thei.html, 2020

19. Theodore Kinni, *Be Our Guest—Perfecting the Art of Customer Service* (Los Angeles, CA: Disney Book Group, 2011)

Chapter 6

1. Theodore Kinni, *Be Our Guest—Perfecting the Art of Customer Service* (Los Angeles, CA: Disney Book Group, 2011).

2. Michael Solomon, *The Heart of Hospitality: Great Hotel and Restaurant Leaders Share Their Secrets* (New York City, NY: Select Books, 2016).

3. https://sharpencx.com/blog/nordstrom-customer-service/

4. Ibid

5. Lauren Cahn, "The real reason Chick-Fil-A employees say my pleasure," 2019, https://www.tasteofhome.com/article/the-real-reason-chick-fil-a-employees-say-my-pleasure/.

6. Chip Bell, "Revive That Old-Fashioned Extra: Good Customer Service," 2014, http://www.entrepreneur.com/232726

7. https://www.qminder.com/use-customer-names/

8. Jason Bordeaux, "What is customer experience, and why is it important?", 2020, https://blog.hubspot.com/service/what-is-customer-experience

9. Justin Macauley, "A Kimpton Moment: Delivering a Great Customer Experience at Every Touchpoint", https://blog.sprinklr.com/great-customer-experience/, 2014

10. Ibid

11. Ibid

12. Ibid

Chapter 7

1. Paul Wadey, "Harlan Howard Obituary", 2002, https://www.independent.co.uk/news/obituaries/harlan-howard-9137791.html

2. Michael Solomon, *The Heart of Hospitality: Great Hotel and Restaurant Leaders Share Their Secrets* (New York City, NY: Select Books, 2016)

3. https://www.helpscout.com/10-customer-service-stories/#two

4. Boyd/Douglas/Tippin, *Working Man's Phd*, (Sony/ATV Music Publishing LLC, Universal Music Publishing Group BMG Rights Management)

5. Donald Trump, *Think Big—Make It Happen in Business and in Life* (Harper House, New York, 2007)

6. Bill Taylor, "Why Zappos pays new employees to quit, and you should too!", 2008, https://hbr.org/2008/05/why-zappos-pays-new-employees

7. Ruth Omoh, "Why Amazon pays employees $5000 to quit", 2018, https://www.cnbc.com/2018/05/21/why-amazon-pays-employees-5000-to-quit.html

Chapter 8

1. Ian Golding, "Whose job is it anyway? The importance of accountability in the world of Customer Experience", 2017, http://customerthink.com/whose-job-is-it-anyway-the-importance-of-accountability-in-the-world-of-customer-experience/

2. Courtney Materano, "How to Incorporate Accountability Into Customer Service", 2018, https://pcgcompanies.com/20181005-incorporating-accountability-to-improve-customer-service/

3. Richard Feloni, "A Zappos employee had the company's longest customer-service call at 10 hours, 43 minutes", 2013, https://www.businessinsider.com/zappos-employee-sets-record-for-longest-customer-service-call-2016-7

4. Michael Solomon, *The Heart of Hospitality: Great Hotel and Restaurant Leaders Share Their Secrets* (New York City, NY: Select Books, 2016)

Afterword

1. Khurana, Simran. "Quotes That Teach Organizations How to Give Respect and Get Respect." ThoughtCo, 2019, thoughtco.com/give-and-get-respect-2830793.

www.ingramcontent.com/pod-product-compliance
Lightning Source LLC
Chambersburg PA
CBHW020658220526
45464CB00001B/491